COLOSSIANS

◆

COLOSSIANS

◆

H. A. IRONSIDE

Revised Edition

Introductory Notes by
John Phillips

LOIZEAUX
Neptune, New Jersey

First Edition, 1929
Revised Edition, 1997

COLOSSIANS
© 1997 by Loizeaux Brothers, Inc.

A Publication of Loizeaux Brothers, Inc.
*A Nonprofit Organization Devoted to the Lord's Work
and to the Spread of His Truth*

Profile taken from *Exploring the Scriptures*
© 1965, 1970, 1989 by John Phillips

Library of Congress Cataloging-in-Publication Data

Ironside, H. A. (Henry Allan), 1876-1951.
Colossians / H. A. Ironside.—Rev.ed. / introductory notes
by John Phillips.
Rev. ed. of: Philippians, Colossians, Thessalonians. 1st ed. 1929.
ISBN 0-87213-419-9 (pbk.: alk. paper)
1. Bible. N.T. Colossians—Commentaries.
I. Ironside, H. A. (Henry Allan), 1876-1951.
Philippians, Colossians, Thessalonians. II. Title.
BS2705.3.I76   1997
227'.7077—dc21   97-2186

Printed in the United States of America
10 9 8 7 6 5 4 3 2 1

CONTENTS

A PROFILE
COLOSSIANS
CHRIST SUPREME

BY JOHN PHILLIPS

Colossians stands in the same relation to Ephesians as Galatians does to Romans. Like Galatians, Colossians is polemic—that is, written to combat error. The error against which Paul warned in Colossians later became known as gnosticism. Besides the gnostic teachings, Jewish ideas were being entertained in the church at Colossae. Paul's answer to this subtle mixture was the supremacy of Christ.

The gnostic heresy, a philosophy based on the notion that matter is evil, concerned itself with the origin of the universe and the nature of evil. The gnostics watered down the gospel to a mere philosophy. Their main goal was to acquire knowledge. On that they put their emphasis, rather than on faith.

The gnostics assumed that since God is good and evil exists, and since (according to their assumption) evil is inherent in matter, God could not have created evil matter. So between God and matter they placed a series of emanations, spirits, and angels. The idea was that one of those spirits came from God, then another spirit came from the first spirit, and so on until there was a spirit far enough away from God to be able to create evil matter without contaminating God. The bottom eon or spirit was called the demiurge.

The god of the gnostics was not the God of the Bible, who according to them was only one of the emanations (see A. T. Robertson, *Paul and the Intellectuals* [rev. ed., Nashville: Broadman, 1959] 10). Confronted with the person of Christ, the gnostics placed Him either at the bottom of the list of spirits or somewhere in the center. In other words, they interpreted Christ in the light of their pagan philosophy. Some denied the humanity of Jesus, but others took an opposite view, maintaining that whereas Jesus was an ordinary man until His baptism, at that time the eon Christ came upon Him and remained with Him until just prior to His death on the cross.

The gnostics' belief that matter was essentially evil caused them to take divergent views of ethical problems. Some argued that since the body was evil it should be subdued, and the result was asceticism. The essenes, and to some extent the stoics, followed that line of reasoning. Others, such as the epicureans, took the view that the only way to overcome sensuality was to indulge bodily cravings to the full, even to excess, exhaustion, and satiety.

Grafted onto the pagan philosophy of gnosticism was a form of pharisaical Judaism. The narrowest view of Jewish ritualism (insisting on circumcision; observance of dietary laws, feasts, and fasts; and the whole cumbersome apparatus of ceremonial religion) was wedded to the original gnostic heresy and presented as truth to the Colossian Christians. The resulting form of "special" knowledge was presented as a mystery—a secret received by revelation rather than scientific deduction, and available only to the initiated. Much of this type of teaching has been revived by present-day cults. In Colossians Paul wrote an inspired "nonsense" across the whole subject.

The Epistle to the Colossians can be outlined in terms of its discussion of the truths about the Christ, the cults, and the Christian.

  I. INTRODUCTION (1:1-14)
 II. THE TRUTH ABOUT THE CHRIST (1:15-29)
     A. The Deity of Christ (1:15-19)
     B. The Death of Christ (1:20-22)
     C. The Demands of Christ (1:23-29)
III. THE TRUTH ABOUT THE CULTS (2:1-23)
     A. We Are to Experience the Truth (2:1-7)
     B. We Are to Expose the Lie (2:8-23)
        1. That Christianity Depends on Secular Reasoning
           (2:8-15)

The Magnificence of Jesus

There are few more magnificent passages in the New Testament than Colossians 1:15-18, where Paul set forth the deity of Christ. The apostle showed that all the divine personality, power, and purposes are centered in Christ.

"All fullness" is in Him (1:19). He is the Creator and Sustainer of the entire universe, yet He died to reconcile men to God and therefore has every right to expect that those who trust in Him will "continue in the faith" and not be "moved away" (1:23).

Paul made known the true mystery: "Christ in you, the hope of glory" (1:27). In the New Testament a mystery is something that can be understood only by the initiated (the saved). To them it is an open secret, a truth once hidden but now revealed, a truth that would have been unknown without special revelation. Paul cut right across the gnostics' pretenses by showing that all true believers are initiated into the true mysteries.

The Claims of the Cults

There are always those who want to add human reasonings to divine revelation. Paul warned the Colossians against intellectualism.

"Beware," he said, "lest any man spoil you through philosophy and vain deceit" (2:8). J. B. Phillips's translation reads, "Be careful that nobody spoils your faith through intellectualism or high-sounding nonsense."

Next Paul attacked the teaching that ritualism would be a good addition to the simplicity of the Christian faith. He showed that the rituals of the law were but "a shadow of things to come" (2:17) and that since the reality had arrived the shadows were superseded. The shadow of a meal cannot satisfy a starving man; the shadow of a key cannot liberate a prisoner. Neither can religious shadows bring peace with God.

Then Paul showed that in talking about "worshipping of angels" (2:18), the gnostics were completely missing Christ. And the apostle demolished the idea that Christianity had anything to gain from rules and regulations, fastings, bodily punishments, and the like. Such things, he said, tended to produce pride rather than perfection.

The Christian Life

As usual Paul turned his attention to practical issues. In the closing chapters of Colossians he discussed the outworkings of proper belief in proper behavior. The Christian, who truly is "risen with Christ," is to set his affections "on things above" and display the life of Christ in every situation as he lives in an evil world (3:1-2). His personal life is to be characterized by purity and love. His spiritual life is to be filled with the Word of God so that songs will ring out from his heart. Everything he does is to be governed by the name of the Lord Jesus.

In domestic life, the Christian is to take the place of wife, husband, child, or parent quietly and radiate Christ. In business relationships the believer—whether employer or employee, master or slave—is to be considerate of the rights of others. In all secular aspects of life the Christian is to act in a way that will cause others to want to become Christians too. His prayers are to be pointed, his time is to be properly invested, and his conversation is to be pungent.

Paul closed the letter by referring to almost a dozen believers dear to him and known to the Colossians. Those men—Tychicus, Onesimus, Aristarchus, Marcus, Justus, Epaphras, Luke, Demas, Nymphas, and Archippus—are well worth getting to know with the aid of a concordance and a Bible dictionary. May our names shine as gloriously in the book of God as most of theirs do! But there's another lesson to be learned from those names. Said Alexander Maclaren:

> There is something very solemn and pathetic in these shadowy names which appear for a moment on the page of Scripture, and are swallowed up of black night, like stars that suddenly blaze out for a week or two, and then dwindle and at last disappear altogether. They too lived and loved and strove and suffered and enjoyed; and now—all is gone, gone; the hot fire burned down to such a little handful of white ashes. Tychicus! Onesimus! two shadows that once were men! And as they are, so we shall be.

INTRODUCTION

No one familiar with the Pauline letters can fail to see that the Epistles to the Ephesians and the Colossians are intimately linked. The apostle was anxious that both should be read by the same people. It is very likely that the letter "from Laodicea" referred to in Colossians 4:16 is really our Epistle to the Ephesians.

Some people who do not accept the inspiration of the New Testament have supposed that Colossians was a crude attempt to rewrite Ephesians from memory, but a careful examination of both letters shows that the one is the correlative of the other.

Ephesians declares the great truth that was revealed to Paul and through him to all nations—the truth that he emphatically called the "mystery." In that letter the apostle presented the church as the body of Christ in its heavenly aspect, just as in 1 Corinthians he set forth the responsibilities of the body down here on the earth. Ephesians of course does not overlook the importance of our responsibility on earth to fulfill our calling and demonstrate the unity of the Spirit. Doctrinally, however, the theme of that Epistle seems to be the body as the aggregate of believers from Pentecost to the rapture, all united to a risen Christ by the indwelling Holy Spirit.

Colossians, on the other hand, has to do with Christ as the Head of the body. This Epistle seeks to fix the hearts of the saints on Him as risen and glorified, known no longer after the flesh but in resurrection as the Head of a new order. And the letter seeks to impress on believers their responsibility in this world to acknowledge Him as the Head of the body. So we might say the headship of Christ is the theme of Colossians.

We should not be surprised to find great similarities in Ephesians and Colossians, for so intimate is the link between Christ and His body that what is said of one may often be said of the other. It is the task of the members of the body to manifest the risen life of the Head. The Holy Spirit focuses our attention on the Head so that we will be separated from all that would dishonor Him and delivered from anything that would tend to keep Him at a distance.

At the beginning of the church age there was an obvious need for ministry such as that found in the book of Colossians. If the Lord Himself had not been watching over His own truth, genuine Christian doctrine might have been overwhelmed in the first centuries by a strange mixture of Jewish legality, Grecian philosophy, and oriental mysticism. These were interwoven to form several altogether new systems of thought with which the name of Christ was linked in a most cunning way. The result was the "mystery of iniquity" referred to in 2 Thessalonians 2:7. The various new systems were grouped under the general name of *gnosticism.*

Gnosticism, at least in title, was the opposite of what Huxley years later designated *agnosticism.* The latter term means "without knowledge." The agnostic claims that God is unknowable, that the mystery of the universe is unsolvable. He says, "There may or may not be a personal God back of this universe; matter may or may not be eternal; man may or may not survive death. I do not know." And he complacently takes it for granted that because he does not know, no one else does. The agnostic refuses to accept the divine revelation given to us in the Holy Scriptures and so is content to be an ignoramus (which is the Latin equivalent of agnostic) when he might have the sure knowledge of one who is taught by God.

The gnostic, on the other hand, said, "I do know." *Gnosis,* from which the term "gnostic" is derived, simply means "knowledge." *Epignosis,* a term used by the apostle to refer to Christianity, really means "superknowledge." The gnostic professed to have fuller knowledge of the mysteries of life and death and heavenly beings than the Bible itself reveals. He added to Scriptural revelation or perverted it by linking it with weird Persian dreams and human reasonings. He was neither a Jew, a Christian, a philosopher, nor a Zoroastrian. The gnostic, having taken what he thought to be the best out of all their systems, considered himself superior to them all, very much as the theosophist does today.

Gnosticism, a weird imitation of the divine mysteries, pretended to great depth of spirituality, remarkable fullness of knowledge, and great profundity of thought. This new system was therefore most attractive to the natural mind, ever delighting in speculation on sacred themes, but it was Satanic in origin and deliberately planned by the enemy to hide the glory shining in the face of Christ Jesus.

I have neither time nor space here to discuss gnosticism's grades of spirit-beings mediating between the uncreated God and His creatures. Those who are interested can readily find full explanations of the demiurge and the host of cabbalistic eons and inferior emanations supposedly coming in between the soul and God. The place that Christ Himself held in this system varied from teacher to teacher; many gnostics indulged in the wildest speculations.

Some thought that Jesus was only a man, and that Christ was the divine Spirit that came to Jesus at His baptism and left Him at the cross; so it could not be said that Christ died—only Jesus died. You will recognize this teaching as the root error of what is commonly called Christian Science. Others held that the body of Jesus was only spiritual, not material; they linked evil with matter and therefore refused to believe that "the Word was made flesh" (John 1:14). The first view seems to have been on the mind of the apostle Paul as he wrote Colossians. The second was addressed by the apostle John in his three Epistles.

Both views rob the saints of the true Christ of God. Gnostic thought puts Him far off with many angels intervening; these must be invoked and placated before union with Christ can be known. Paul showed that we can come to Him immediately, that the man Christ Jesus is the "one mediator between God and men" (1 Timothy 2:5). The gnostics placed Christ below various ranks of principalities and powers and glorious spirit-beings leading up to the invisible God, whereas Paul showed that Christ is the Creator of all principalities and powers and that they must all be subject to Him "who is the image of the invisible God" (Colossians 1:15).

I would not think it necessary to discuss these old errors if it were not true that the danger of losing sight of the Head is as real today as it was in Paul's day. Every modern erroneous cult is just some old Satanic heresy revived, and each is designed to misrepresent some aspect of revealed truth about Christ and His redemptive work. The advocates of these systems may profess great humility and preach and practice great self-abnegation, even to the point of neglecting the body and its physical needs. But they all put Christ Jesus, the true Christ of God, at a distance and set an imaginary christ, a christ who is not an atoning savior, in His place. Some degree of familiarity with the ancient theories might prevent honest souls from being entangled in the meshes of the newer systems. Therefore Christians of every era need to read this Colossian letter so that they will hold onto the concept of Christ as Head of the body.

It has been observed by others, but it bears repeating, that the Spirit is so intent on glorifying Christ in this wonderful Epistle that He hides Himself. In Ephesians, where the truth of the one body is being unfolded, the Holy Spirit is mentioned many times and we find clear teaching as to His personality and function. But in Colossians He is never mentioned doctrinally, and only once "incidentally" (I do not mean without divine design) and that is in 1:8 where Paul referred to his readers' "love in the Spirit." This omission is surely most significant. The Holy Spirit, though eternally coequal with the Father and Son who all together constitute one God, hides Himself lest men belittle or lose sight of the Lord Jesus as Head of the new creation. The blessed Paraclete speaks not of Himself, but shows the things of Christ to us. He would not even "risk" (as men would say) being thought of as One coming between the believer and Christ.

As far as we know, Paul had never been to Colossae as a ministering servant, although Philemon, who was a resident of that city, had been converted through him. The apostle had not seen the saints to whom he was writing, but many of them may have heard him during the time he was in Ephesus when "all they which dwelt in Asia heard the word" (Acts 19:10). "Asia" here refers not to the continent nor to Asia Minor, but to a much smaller district ruled by a Roman proconsul and therefore known as the "proconsular province of Asia." At one time Paul was forbidden to go to Asia, but later he labored there with much blessing. The seven churches of the Apocalypse were located in Asia. Although Colossae was not addressed by the Lord when He appeared to John in Patmos, the city was situated close to Laodicea, which with Colossae and Hierapolis formed a trio of cities with large assemblies of Christians in the early days.

Epaphras was the chosen instrument for the evangelization of Colossae. He evidently remained among the saints and cared for them as a godly pastor after their conversion. But he was beset by emissaries of Satan who for their own selfish advantage were bent on misleading the young believers. Epaphras therefore sought the help of the apostle Paul, who at the time was a prisoner in Rome. In response to this pastor's plea, Paul—by divine inspiration—penned his letter to the Colossians.

In so many instances God permitted error in doctrine or corruption in life in the early churches to be the means of adding to the volume of divine revelation and instruction. In His mercy and wisdom He allowed every possible form of error to arise in the apostolic era of the church's history so that all error might be exposed and the truth declared through inspired men, thus preserving the faith in its simplicity for the generations to come. As a result Satan has nothing new to offer.

From time to time old heresies are re-dressed and introduced as new conceptions of truth, but "there is no new thing under the sun" (Ecclesiastes 1:9). All the Christian needs to protect him from modern evil systems of thought is a better acquaintance with the Word of God. In Scripture the truth is taught in its purity and the lies of the adversary are brought out into the light and fully exposed. No one familiar with the teaching of Colossians, for instance, will ever be misled by the specious sophistries of the various occult systems now being foisted on a credulous public. He will not be misled by theosophy or spiritualism, nor will he be deluded by the revived gnostic religions of Eddyism, the Unity School of Christianity, or other branches of the misnamed New Thought.

The first part of Colossians is doctrinal (1:1–3:4) and the second part is practical (3:5 – 4:18). This letter is a precious portion of the Word of God and, like all Scripture, was "written for our learning" (Romans 15:4). The Epistle seems to have increasing value as new cults and false systems abound, for they are all designed to make us lose sight of the Head and forget our union with Him in glory.

CHAPTER ONE
CHRIST, THE HEAD OF THE BODY

Salutation (Colossians 1:1-2)

The Epistle to the Colossians opens with these words: "Paul, an apostle of Jesus Christ by the will of God, and Timotheus our brother."

Thirteen Epistles in the New Testament begin with the name "Paul." A fourteenth letter, in spite of considerable dispute about its authorship, is generally accepted as having come from the same pen; that letter is the Epistle to the Hebrews. But the opening word of that Epistle is "God." The thirteen beginning with the word "Paul" are addressed either to churches among the Gentiles or to individual believers. Paul was the apostle to the Gentiles and as such he magnified his office. But he was not the apostle to the Hebrews and if he was the one chosen to write the Epistle to the Hebrews (as I firmly believe he was), it was quite in keeping with his Gentile apostleship that he should hide his name in that wonderful exposition of the old and new covenants. Christ alone was the Apostle and Prophet of the new covenant, as Moses and Aaron had been of the old, and so the opening word of Hebrews is simply "God"—"God, who...hath in these last days spoken unto us by his Son" (Hebrews 1:1-2).

In the Colossian letter Paul associated himself with Timothy in the salutation. The bond between these two men of God, far apart in age though they were, was a very real one. Timothy was converted during Paul's ministry at Lystra, and when the apostle next visited the same region, the brethren heartily commended the young man to him. In their judgment Timothy was a believer who, because of his spiritual graces and gifts, was suited to go out in the ministry of the Word. Acting on their advice, Paul took Timothy with him after the elder brethren had solemnly laid their hands on him and commended him to God for this special service.

Throughout the years that followed, Timothy proved himself in every respect to be reliable and devoted. His unselfish concern for the welfare of the people of God and his loyal attachment to his human leader endeared him to the venerable apostle. It seems that Timothy even accompanied Paul to Rome, or followed him there, and was either sharing his imprisonment or living nearby so that he could alleviate the suffering of the apostle as well as minister to the Roman believers. So in the salutation Paul connected the young preacher with himself when he sent his greetings to the saints at Colossae.

Paul attributed his own apostleship directly to the will of God. It was He who had revealed Christ both to and in him, had set him apart for service, and had commissioned him to proclaim the unsearchable riches of grace among the Gentiles. It would be preposterous to suppose that the laying on of hands by the church at Antioch (Acts 13:3) conferred any authority whatever on either Barnabas or Paul, inasmuch as they had been approved laborers in the gospel for some time. The laying on of hands simply expressed, as in Timothy's case, the fellowship of a local assembly of Christians. It was the Holy Spirit who sent forth Barnabas and Paul and ordained them. So we read that Paul was an apostle "by the will of God" (Colossians 1:1).

Writing to the Galatians, Paul used similar expressions, calling himself an apostle "not of men, neither by man, but by Jesus Christ, and God the Father" (Galatians 1:1). He was stating a principle of far-reaching importance in connection with the work of the ministry. Whenever men presume to add anything to the divine call or to confer authority on a servant of Christ, they are usurping the place of the Holy Spirit. The most that any laying on of hands can do is to express fellowship in the work.

In Colossians 1:2 the Christians at Colossae are addressed as the "saints and faithful brethren." These words do not indicate that there are two classes of believers. Rather, the expression "saints" suggests the divine call, while the expression "faithful brethren" suggests the human response.

It is God who designates His redeemed ones as "saints," yet Romanists and many Protestants are generally mistaken about the meaning of the term. Romanists think that a saint is a particularly holy person who displays great devotion or possesses miraculous powers and is included on the list of intermediaries credited with a superabundance of merit or goodness that may be appropriated by others. Many who profess to have greater enlightenment than the Romanists, think that a saint is one who has become victorious in the struggle with sin and has been received triumphantly into Heaven; so they speak of the Christian dead as "sainted." But the Scriptural concept is altogether different. The vilest sinner is constituted a saint by God the moment he puts his trust in the Lord Jesus Christ, "who was delivered for our offences, and was raised again for our justification" (Romans 4:25). Thus we are saints by calling and not primarily by practice.

However, we should be careful not to divorce the practical side of truth from the doctrinal. Being saints, we are now responsible to live in a saintly way. In other words, we are to live out practically what God has already declared to be true of us doctrinally. We do not become saints by the display of saintly virtues; but because we are saints, we are to cultivate saintly character traits. This of course is done in communion with God and in obedience to His Word as we walk in the power of the Holy Spirit.

The expression "faithful brethren" follows the expression "saints" but does not, I take it, refer to a higher class of believers. "Faithful brethren" are brethren who believe. As we read elsewhere, "They which be of faith are blessed with faithful Abraham" (Galatians 3:9). The verse might also be translated, "They that have faith are blessed with faithful Abraham," or "They that believe are blessed with believing Abraham." All real Christians are believing or faithful brethren. Those who profess to be Christ's but do not believe His Word show themselves to be unreal and false to their profession, for it is written, "He that cometh to God must believe that he is, and that he is a rewarder of them that diligently seek him"

(Hebrews 11:6). We are also told, "If ye continue in my word, then are ye my disciples indeed" (John 8:31).

Colossians 1:2 continues with the usual apostolic greeting: "Grace be unto you, and peace, from God our Father and the Lord Jesus Christ." Grace is God's free unmerited favor. It is even more than that. It is favor against merit. When we merit the very opposite, God lavishes His lovingkindness on us. That is grace. He who sits on a throne of grace bids us come boldly to obtain grace and mercy as daily needs arise, and we gladly echo the words of the hymn: "Since our souls have known His love, / What mercies has He made us prove!"

The peace Paul spoke of here is the peace of God that surrounds and protects His people's hearts in the day of evil. We have this peace amid the most disquieting circumstances because we are assured that "all things work together for good to them that love God, to them who are the called according to his purpose" (Romans 8:28).

Introduction (Colossians 1:3-6)

We are reminded of the introduction to the Epistle to the Ephesians as we read this Colossian passage, which begins with an expression of thanksgiving to "God and the Father of our Lord Jesus Christ" (Colossians 1:3). God is thus presented as both Creator and Savior, for it is through Jesus Christ that our salvation is mediated.

Having heard of the conversion of the Colossians, the apostle was stirred to pray on their behalf. Whenever he learned of more people coming to Christ, his burden of prayer was invariably increased. Paul felt, with an intensity that few men have felt, the great need of intercession for the people of God. He knew well the fearful opposition that Satan, the prince and god of this world, directs toward those who trust in the Lord Jesus Christ, and he realized the prevailing power of prayer to defeat the adversary. Therefore Paul bowed in the presence of God in earnest supplication on behalf of those whom grace had saved.

Notice how faith, love, and hope are linked together in Colossians 1:4-5, as in so many other places in Scripture. The order is different in 1 Corinthians 13. There, where Paul was exalting love, he put faith first, hope second, and love last—to indicate that love will remain when the other two have passed away. But in Colossians 1 he put faith first, love second, and hope last: hope closes the life that begins with faith, and the two are linked by love. Faith claims salvation at the cross. Hope looks ahead to Heaven. Love is the power that motivates the saint in the interim.

The Colossians had trusted their souls to a divine person. Sometimes people are troubled by the fear that their faith is not of the right quality or that it is of insufficient quantity to save them. But it is important to observe that it is not the character of faith or the amount of faith that saves. It is the person in whom faith rests that saves. The strongest faith in self-effort, or in the church, or in religious observances would leave the soul forever lost. But the feeblest faith in the Christ who died and rose again, saves eternally. Some people try to make a savior of their faith, but Christ alone is the Savior and faith but the hand that reaches out to Him.

Paul spoke of the love that the Colossians had "to all the saints." Such love is precious indeed. It is the evidence of the divine nature imparted in the new birth and the evidence of the indwelling of the Holy Spirit. The very nature of the born-again soul is to love not only God, but also those who are begotten of Him. This love, which knows no sectarian limitation, embraces all the people of God.

The Colossians looked to the future because they had heard before of the hope of Heaven. No one fully preaches the gospel who leaves out the truth of the blessed hope of the Lord's return to receive His people to be with Himself in the Father's house. This is the glad consummation of the believer's life of faith, love, and hope. The gospel does not set death before the believer as his hope; the gospel always declares that it is the Lord's return for which he is to wait.

The gospel is God's good news about His Son and therefore, when fully preached, necessarily includes the proclamation of His true sinless humanity, His deity, His virgin birth, His vicarious sacrifice, His glorious resurrection, His present role as Advocate and High Priest at God's right hand in Heaven, and His coming again to reign in power and righteousness when all His redeemed will be associated with Him. All these precious truths are included "in the word of the truth of the gospel."

In Colossians 1:6 we learn that this gospel, even in Paul's day, had been carried to the ends of the earth. The same message that had reached Colossae had been preached in all the world, as 1:23 also declares. And wherever this evangel of the cross had gone, it had produced fruit to the praise and glory of God in those who believed it.

It is the height of folly to look for fruit before the soul has made peace with God or to expect evidence of salvation in the life before the gospel has been believed. Salvation is altogether a work of grace. Human effort has no place in it at all. Neither are we saved by the work of the Spirit, who produces the nine fruits mentioned in Galatians 5:22-23. We are saved by the work of Christ—a work done for us but altogether outside of us, a work in which we had no part except that we committed the sins that put the Savior on the cross. An uneducated old man said, "I did my part and God did His: I did the sinning and God did the saving. I took to running away from Him as fast as my sins could carry me and He took after me until He run me down!" Others might express this truth more elegantly, but no one could express it more correctly and clearly.

The gospel is a message to be believed, not a collection of precepts or a code of laws to be obeyed. Salvation is of faith that it might be by grace, "not of works, lest any man should boast" (Ephesians 2:9). The moment the message is believed it produces new life in the soul. The Spirit comes to dwell within the believer and this invariably results in precious fruit for God. This was the experience of the Colossian believers. The gospel message brought forth fruit in their lives after they "heard...and knew the grace of God in truth." (Note that in the King James version of Colossians 1:6 it would have been better to omit the italicized words *of it*.)

Epaphras's Report (Colossians 1:7-8)

The gospel message had not been carried to Colossae by the apostle Paul, for as far as we know he had never visited that city as a messenger of the cross (see Colossians 2:1). It was another devoted man of God, Epaphras by name, who had proclaimed the gospel to the Colossians. Paul spoke of him affectionately as "our dear fellowservant" and declared that he was "a faithful minister of Christ" (1:7). We gather from 4:12 that Epaphras's outstanding characteristic was his fervency in prayer. How blessed we are when faithful preaching and fervent prayer go together! Unfortunately they are often divorced.

In Colossians 1:8 we find the only reference to the Holy Spirit in this Epistle. When the truth about Christ as the Head of the church is being questioned or when Satan is seeking to interpose anything between the soul and Christ, God will not even draw the attention of the saints to the person or work of the Spirit, lest by preoccupation with subjective truth they lose sight of the great objective verities. So here the reference to the Spirit is only incidental. Paul simply mentioned the fact that Epaphras had told him and Timothy of the Colossians' "love in the Spirit."

Epaphras's report was a precious testimony to the happy state of these dear young Christians so recently brought out of paganism with all its abominations. Now as a company set apart for the Lord Jesus Christ, they were characterized by that love which the Spirit sheds abroad in the hearts of those who are born of God.

"Love in the Spirit" is all-important. To pretend to be zealous for the truth of the one body while failing to demonstrate the love of the Spirit, is to put the emphasis in the wrong place. Doctrinal correctness will never atone for lack of brotherly love. It means far more to God, who is Himself love in His very nature, that His people walk in love toward one another than that they contend valiantly for doctrinal systems, however Scriptural they may be. "Truthing in love" (an expression that would correctly convey the thought of Ephesians 4:15) involves more than contending for one's interpretation of the truth. What Paul had in mind included the exemplification of the truth in a life of love for God and for those who are His—as well as for poor lost sinners for whom Christ died.

Paul's Prayer (Colossians 1:9-14)

This passage reminds us of the prayers of the apostle for the Ephesians, as recorded in chapters 1 and 3 of that Epistle. There is something very precious and exceedingly instructive in being permitted to share Paul's thoughts about the Lord's people in Colossae and to read his petitions for them in their various circumstances. His deep concern—for their growth in grace, for their enlightenment in divine things, for their understanding of the purpose of God, for the evidence of spiritual power in their lives—was strikingly revealed as he bowed his knees before the God and Father of our Lord Jesus Christ. The apostle was not content to know people were justified and hence safe for eternity.

Paul was controlled by the earnest desire that all the Colossians would understand their calling so that their life and walk might be in harmony with it. The apostle wanted them to remember that they were here to represent Christ, their risen Head. These desires formed the burden of his prayers. It is doubtful that any merely human writer has ever given suggestions as helpful as the thoughts that will come to us about our own prayer lives as we meditate on Paul's petitions.

In Colossians 1:12-14 the apostle gave thanks for certain blessings that are non-forfeitable because they are bestowed on us by God at the moment we believe on Christ who died to make them ours. But in verses 9-11 Paul asked for certain other additional blessings for which we need to pray daily; we need to exercise our souls constantly lest we fail to experience these benefits. It is very important to distinguish between the two classes of blessings, but many believers fail to make the distinction.

In certain circles almost every public prayer is concluded somewhat as follows: "We pray Thee, forgive us our sins, and wash us in the blood of Jesus. Receive us into Thy kingdom, give us Thy Holy Spirit, and save us at last for Christ's sake. Amen." Yet every petition in this prayer has already been granted to the believer in Christ! God has forgiven all trespasses. We have been cleansed by the blood of Jesus. He has moved us out of the kingdom of darkness into the kingdom of the Son of His love. He has sealed us with His Holy Spirit, for "if any man have not the Spirit of Christ, he is none of his" (Romans 8:9). Since we are saved eternally from the moment we believe the gospel, we might far rather cry exultantly in faith: "We thank Thee that Thou hast forgiven all our sins and washed every stain in the blood of the Lamb. Thou hast brought us into Thy kingdom, given us Thy Holy Spirit, and saved us for eternity." Faith says amen to what God has declared in His Word to be true. To go on praying for blessings that He tells us are already ours is the most subtle kind of unbelief and robs us of the enjoyment that could be our portion if we had faith to believe the "exceeding great and precious promises" that are ours in Christ (2 Peter 1:4).

Let us therefore follow the apostle's prayer carefully, weighing every phrase and clause, and distinguishing between petition and thanksgiving. His petitions begin in Colossians 1:9, where he told his readers that he prayed that they "might be filled with the knowledge of [God's] will." Those who were troubling the Colossian saints boasted of their superior knowledge. These gnostics had evolved a complex system of mystical and wholly imaginative teaching regarding the soul's approach to God through an interminable number of intermediaries; they coupled this teaching with ascetic regulations and legal observances. In their eyes the gospel as preached by Paul was simplicity indeed; they looked on it as a child's conception of the philosophy of the universe; they viewed the gospel as puerile for men of mature minds. But he who knew this gospel in all its grandeur, as few other men have ever known it, spoke here of being "filled with the *knowledge* of [God's] will" (italics added); and he used a superlative instead of a word that the gnostics were very fond of. They boasted of *gnosis,* which means "knowledge," but he said *epignosis,* which literally means "superknowledge." It is in the divine revelation alone that this is found.

When Paul used the expression "the knowledge of his will" here, I do not think he was referring merely to God's will for the individual believer's life from day to day, although that would indeed be involved in the broader concept, just as a drop of water is included in the ocean. I think the apostle was referring to the Father's wondrous plan that has been known from eternity, is now being carried out in time, and will have its consummation in the ages to come. Knowledge of this eternal purpose of God is superknowledge indeed! The cleverest human intellect could never fathom it, apart from divine revelation.

This revelation we have in our Bibles. Running throughout the Scriptures from Genesis to the Apocalypse, it furnishes a theme for devout contemplation, demands enthusiastic study and careful examination by the most erudite minds and brilliant intellects, and calls for the deepest investigation of the most spiritual believers. At the same time, unlearned and ignorant Christians will find constant enjoyment in this revelation if they allow themselves to be guided by the Spirit in searching the Scriptures for knowledge of God's will.

Paul understood the important fact that truth is not learned through the intellect alone, so he prayed that the Colossians might comprehend God's eternal purpose "in all wisdom and spiritual understanding." Wisdom, which is the ability to use knowledge correctly, is imparted by the Spirit; He alone gives true understanding. The mind of God as revealed in His Word can be comprehended when there is subjection of heart to the divine Teacher and when there is that self-judgment and self-distrust which lead one to walk softly before God—not in self-will or egotism, but in humility and lowly dependence on the One who inspired the Holy Scriptures, which alone can make the simple wise.

God opens up His truth to us so that we may delight in the wondrous things He has revealed and so that we may walk in the power of the knowledge He has given. So Paul prayed that his readers "might walk worthy of the Lord" (Colossians 1:10). We can only "walk worthy of the Lord" as we know His mind. The study of His Word and a godly walk should always go together.

It is noteworthy that in Ephesians 4:1 we are exhorted to "walk worthy of [our] vocation [calling]" as members of the body of Christ; in Philippians 1:27 we are told to walk "as it becometh the gospel" (or "worthy of the gospel"), which we are left in the world to proclaim; and in 1 Thessalonians 2:12 we are bidden to "walk worthy of God," who has called us to His kingdom and glory. We are always to walk according to the truth that has been revealed to our souls, so in Colossians the thought is that we are to "walk worthy of the Lord," who is the Head of the new creation to which we now belong.

We are to "walk worthy of the Lord unto all pleasing." Dr. Griffith Thomas pointed out that the Greek word rendered "pleasing" here is not found in any other passage in the New Testament, but is used elsewhere to mean "a preference of the will of others before our own." The phrase translated "unto all pleasing" in the King James version was rendered by Bishop Handley Moule as "unto every anticipation of His will."

We are blessed indeed when the will of God is sweeter far to us than our own will and we delight in doing His will, not to gain His favor, but to give joy to His heart. Yet most of us learn so slowly that the only true happiness in life is to be found in doing the will of God. In vain we seek for satisfaction by trying to get our own way until at last, like a bird wearied by flying against the bars of its cage, we fall back on the will of God and learn that in it the mind and heart find perfect rest. Then we say with the hymn writer:

> O the peace my Savior gives,
> Peace I never knew before!
> And my way has brighter grown
> Since I learned to trust Him more.
> (F. A. Blackmer)

The believer who delights in doing the will of God becomes fruitful. The expression Paul used in Colossians 1:10 is translated "being fruitful in every good work" in the King James version. A better rendering might be "bearing fruit in every good work."

The phrase "every good work" should not make us think simply of preaching the gospel, teaching the Holy Scriptures, or engaging in what is sometimes called Christian activity or church work. We are prone to distinguish between secular and sacred employment, but everything in a believer's life is sacred. We need to be reminded of this over and over again. The Church of Rome recognizes seven sacraments, but every act of a Christian should be sacramental, using the word as generally understood. Whatever is right and proper for me to do in any circumstance, I should do with the one purpose of bringing glory to God; by so doing I will be bearing fruit for Him.

The testimony of one little maid has gone around the world. She said, "I know I am converted, and my mistress knows I am converted, because I clean under the rug now." Wherever the gospel is preached, her story is told "for a memorial of her" (Matthew 26:13). Even in the most commonplace duties she was bearing fruit for God as she sought to glorify Him by the faithful performance of her responsibilities. She did her chores "not with eyeservice, as menpleasers" (Colossians 3:22), "not as pleasing men, but God, which trieth our hearts" (1 Thessalonians 2:4).

As we walk with God from day to day, we increase in our knowledge of Him. This is more than knowledge of the Word of God, although undoubtedly the one leads to the other, for God has made Himself known through His Word. "Increasing in the knowledge of God" (Colossians 1:10) means learning more of His love and grace, His tender compassion, and His care for those who trust Him—and proving how solemn a thing it is to deviate from the path of obedience and thus be exposed to the rod of correction. We know God as we walk with Him; we walk with Him as we obey His Word.

> We know Him as we could not know
> Through Heaven's golden years;
> We there shall see His glorious face,
> On earth we see His tears.
>
> The touch that heals the broken heart
> Is never felt above;
> His angels know His blessedness,
> His way-worn saints His love.

Every trial along our pilgrim path gives God a new opportunity to reveal His heart to us, His needy people who are so dependent on His power and grace. We will thank Him through all eternity for these chances to increase in our knowledge of Him.

As we walk with God, we are "strengthened with all might, according to his glorious power" (Colossians 1:11). God supplies strength and gives us all the power we need to overcome in every adverse circumstance. What room is there for discouragement as temptations and trials surround us and seem about to overwhelm us, if we realize that the same spiritual dynamic, the same wondrous energy which raised Christ from the dead operates in us by the Spirit? I can be more than victorious through Him who loves me!

It may seem to you that all this expenditure of divine energy would result in a great outward display that would astonish and amaze an unbelieving world. But it doesn't. We are strengthened "unto all patience and longsuffering." We need this dynamic force to keep our hearts in subjection to God's will so that we can patiently bear whatever He in His wisdom sees fit to let us go through while we are in this wilderness world. We do not simply endure with the stoical resignation that a pagan philosopher might exhibit. Instead we patiently wait on God and rest in His love; we exhibit longsuffering (uncomplaining endurance) even amid difficult circumstances.

But we do even more: we display "joyfulness." In the hour of trial a song of gladness wells up in the heart where the will of God is supreme. The natural man knows nothing of joy in the time of trial; gladness in the time of hardship; songs in the night though the darkness be overwhelming; praises to God when nature shrinks and trembles. God's glorious power enabled the martyrs to rejoice in the arena when they were thrown to the lions and to exult in the Lord when flames leaped up around them at the stake. All through the Christian era a myriad of sufferers have been able to testify to the sustaining grace of God when their spirits seemed about to be overwhelmed. They experienced the truth of the words of Nehemiah 8:10: "The joy of the Lord is your strength."

Having presented his petitions to the Lord in Colossians 1:9-11, Paul turned to thanksgiving in 1:12-14. Verses 12-14 are in marked contrast to verses 9-11. In verses 12-14 all is positive and eternally settled. The blessings enumerated are ours from the moment we believe in the Lord Jesus Christ and are absolutely irrevocable. To ask for them would be to dishonor God by casting doubt on His Word. Notice the three *haths* and the one *have* in the King James version; these words speak of present possession. Faith lays hold of such statements in Scripture and rejoices in the assurance that these wondrous blessings are to be enjoyed even now.

In Colossians 1:12 we read that the Father "hath made us meet [fit] to be partakers of the inheritance of the saints in light." This refers to every Christian, for there are no degrees in this divine fitness. We are made fit to partake of our glorious inheritance the instant we are cleansed from our sins and receive the new nature, which is divinely imparted when we are born of God. How different are man's thoughts about fitness! Even some of the best of men have been heard to say of a devoted and aged believer, "He is fit for Heaven at last." But he was just as fit for Heaven the moment he received Christ as he is at the end of a long life of devoted service. Fitness does not depend on experience.

However, we need to remember that there is something more than the Father's house ("the inheritance of the saints") in our future. It is also important to keep in mind the coming glorious kingdom. Peter told us how we are fitted for a place in that kingdom. In 2 Peter 1:5-7 he enumerated various Christian virtues and then referred to them as "these things" in verses 10 and 11: "Give diligence to make your calling and election sure: for if ye do *these things,* ye shall never fall: For so an entrance shall be ministered unto you abundantly into the everlasting kingdom of our Lord and Saviour Jesus Christ" (italics added). So we fit ourselves for the coming kingdom by adding "these things" to our faith, but it is the justifying, regenerating grace of God that makes us fit for our heavenly inheritance. In other words, we need to distinguish between salvation by grace and reward for service.

In Colossians 1:13 we read of a kingdom that is different from the one mentioned in 2 Peter 1:11. Paul said that the Father "hath delivered us from the power [or authority] of darkness, and hath translated us into the kingdom of his dear Son." This kingdom is the present sphere where Christ's authority is acknowledged, the kingdom that we see and enter by new birth, the kingdom that consists not of "meat and drink; but righteousness, and peace, and joy in the Holy Ghost" (Romans 14:17).

When we are born of God, we lose our old standing as sons of fallen Adam in the Satanic kingdom of darkness. We are brought out of the darkness into the marvelous light of the children of God (1 Peter 2:9), and of course we therefore have the responsibility to "walk as children of light" (Ephesians 5:8). J. N. Darby was once asked, "Suppose a Christian turns his back on the light; what then?"

He replied, "Then the light will shine upon his back." What a blessing it is to comprehend this truth! We are in the light by virtue of the precious atoning blood of our Lord Jesus Christ, which has been sprinkled on the mercyseat, the very throne of God from which the light shines.

In Colossians 1:14 we read that in Christ "we have redemption through his blood, even the forgiveness of sins." There is some question about whether the expression "through his blood" occurred in the original Epistle. The phrase seems to have been copied from the parallel passage in Ephesians 1:7. The best editors generally omit the phrase from Colossians 1:14, but that does not for one moment alter the truth we have been considering. Omitting "through his blood" would only suggest the fuller character of redemption, which is by both blood and power. The blood having been shed, the omnipotent power of God makes redemption real to the believer, whose sins have all been forgiven and who has been lifted completely out of those circumstances in which he was exposed to the judgment of God.

The wonderful truths so succinctly presented in Colossians 1:12-14 are blessed certainties that tell in unmistakable terms of our eternal security once we are in Christ. As the soul meditates on these verses, the heart will surely reach out to God in worship and the life will be yielded for devoted service.

Christ the Firstborn (Colossians 1:15-19)

Having considered the role of our Lord Jesus as God's dear Son in whom we have redemption, we now direct our attention to His role as the One who has made God known to us. He has come into the world as a man who is "the image of the invisible God" (Colossians 1:15)—the God who the gnostics said could never be known or understood! John 1:18 says, "No man hath seen God at any time; the only begotten Son, which is in the bosom of the Father, he hath declared him."

Five times in the New Testament the Son is called the "only begotten." This endearing term, which always refers to what He has been throughout eternity, implies unity in life and nature. In

Hebrews 11:17 Isaac is called Abraham's "only begotten son," yet Ishmael was also his son. But the link between Abraham and Isaac was of a unique character. And so as the "only begotten," our Lord is the unique Son. He has been that eternally, for if He were not the eternal Son, God would not be the eternal Father.

God has existed throughout eternity as three persons—Father, Son, and Holy Spirit—but He never became visible to created eyes, whether of angels or men, until the holy babe was born in Bethlehem. The Son was as truly the invisible God as the Father or the Spirit was—until the incarnation. Then He was seen by angels and later on by men. As born of a virgin mother without any human father, He is the Son of God in a new sense, and it is as such He is acknowledged by the Father as "the firstborn of every creature" (Colossians 1:15). Perhaps a better rendering would be "the firstborn of all creation." Paul was not implying that the Son is created; he meant that He is the Head of all that has been created.

So we see that the title "firstborn" is not to be understood solely as a divine title, although He who bears the name is divine. But it is as man that He is acknowledged by God the Father as the Firstborn, as the Head of all creation. And how right it is that such a title should be conferred on Him, for "by him were all things created" (Colossians 1:16). Coming into the world as man, He took that title because of the dignity of His person. His is the glory of the Firstborn because He is the Creator. The Firstborn is the heir and pre-eminent One.

It is important to remember that in Scripture the firstborn is not necessarily the one born first. In many instances the one born first was set aside and the rights of the firstborn were given to another. In the cases of Ishmael and Isaac, Esau and Jacob, Reuben and Joseph, Manasseh and Ephraim, for example, the first man was set aside and the second man was acknowledged as the firstborn. And so Adam and all his race are set aside as unfit to retain authority over the world so that the Second Man, Christ the Lord from Heaven, may be acknowledged as the Firstborn.

We can see how these truths would contradict the gnostic conception of a *created* Jesus to whom the Christ, a divine emanation, came at baptism, only to leave Him again at Calvary. It was the *eternal* Son who stooped in grace to become the Son of God in a new sense when he was born of a virgin. We should never lose sight of the fact that His sonship is spoken of in these two distinct ways in Scripture. As the eternal Son preincarnate, he is called the Son, the Son of the Father, and the Son of God, but the third term generally refers to what He became when He joined His deity with humanity. He became God and man in one person with two natures, fulfilling the words the angel had addressed to His virgin mother: "That holy thing which shall be born of thee shall be called the Son of God" (Luke 1:35).

When we consider this great mystery, we must be very accurate in our thinking and not let our thoughts run beyond Holy Scripture. Let us consider some of the passages that deal with the sonship of Christ. It was of the virgin-born Savior that Micah prophesied: "Bethlehem Ephratah, though thou be little among the thousands of Judah, yet out of thee shall he come forth unto me that is to be ruler in Israel; whose goings forth have been from of old, from everlasting [from the days of eternity]"(Micah 5:2). If carefully weighed, the five passages in which Christ is called the "only begotten" will make Micah's prophecy clear:

> The Word became flesh and tabernacled among us, and we beheld His glory (the glory as of the only begotten of the Father), full of grace and truth (John 1:14, literal rendering).

> No man hath seen God at any time; the only begotten Son, subsisting in the bosom of the Father, He hath told Him out (John 1:18, literal rendering).

> God so loved the world, that he gave his only begotten Son, that whosoever believeth in him should not perish, but have everlasting life (John 3:16).

> He that believeth on him is not condemned: but he that believeth not is condemned already, because he hath not believed in the name of the only begotten Son of God (John 3:18).

In this was manifested the love of God toward us, because that God sent his only begotten Son into the world, that we might live through him (1 John 4:9).

In five other passages Christ is called the "firstborn" or "first begotten":

Who is the image of the invisible God, the firstborn of every creature [or, of all creation] (Colossians 1:15).

He is the head of the body, the church: who is the beginning, the firstborn from the dead; that in all things he might have the pre-eminence (Colossians 1:18).

For whom he did foreknow, he also did predestinate to be conformed to the image of his Son, that he might be the firstborn among many brethren (Romans 8:29).

Jesus Christ, who is the faithful witness, and the first begotten of [or, from among] the dead, and the prince of the kings of the earth (Revelation 1:5).

When He bringeth the firstborn into the habitable earth, again He saith, And let all the angels of God worship Him (Hebrews 1:6, literal rendering).

Colossians 1:16 tells us that the Son brought all things into being. "Without him was not any thing made that was made" (John 1:3). All the inhabitants of Heaven and earth owe their life to Him. All "visible and invisible" beings are the creatures of His hand. Angels, no matter how great their dignity—"whether they be thrones, or dominions, or principalities, or powers"—were all created by Him and for His glory. The gnostics placed these varied ranks of exalted beings between Christ and God, but Christ is superior to them all, for He brought them into being. He is the uncreated Son who became man to accomplish the work of redemption. Higher than all angels, He was made a little lower than they "for the suffering of death" (Hebrews 2:9).

Colossians 1:17 insists on Christ's pre-eminence in another way. Paul wrote, "He is before all things." Christ existed as the eternal Word before all personal and impersonal created things existed. "In the beginning was the Word, and the Word was with God, and the Word was God" (John 1:1). John was ascribing to Christ full deity, yet distinct personality.

Colossians 1:17 continues, "By him all things consist [hold together]." It is Christ who sustains the universe. His hand holds the stars in their courses, directs the planets in their orbits, and controls the laws of the universe. How great is His dignity and how low did He stoop for our salvation!

But men rejected Him. They said, "This is the heir; come, let us kill him, that the inheritance may be ours" (Luke 20:14), and they slew Him by hanging Him on a tree. It was then that God made Christ's soul an offering for sin and He accomplished the great work of redemption for which He came to earth. The Just suffered for the unjust "that he might bring us to God" (1 Peter 3:18), but having died for our offenses, Christ "was raised again for our justification" (Romans 4:25). Thus He became the Firstborn in a new sense; as "the firstborn from the dead" he became the Head of the new creation (Colossians 1:18).

There was no union with Christ in His incarnation; union is in resurrection. He was alone as the incarnate Son on earth; it is after His resurrection that He is hailed as the Firstborn from among the dead. As Christ Himself said, "Except a corn of wheat fall into the ground and die, it abideth alone: but if it die, it bringeth forth much fruit" (John 12:24). In resurrection He becomes "the head of the body, the church" and "the beginning" of the creation of God (Colossians 1:18); "the firstborn among many brethren" (Romans 8:29); the resurrection King-Priest; the One who is yet to rule the world in glory; the Melchizedek of the age to come, as the book of Hebrews shows us.

Colossians 1:19 is difficult to translate euphoniously, and in our King James version the words "the Father" have been added in order to complete what seems like an incomplete sentence: "It pleased the Father that in him should all fulness dwell." But it should be carefully noted that there is no term in the original Epistle that could be translated "the Father." The original indicates that it was "the fullness" that was pleased to dwell in Jesus. If we connect this verse with Colossians 2:9 we understand at once what Paul had in mind. There he wrote, "In him dwelleth all the fulness of the Godhead bodily." So Colossians 1:19 must mean, "In Him all the fullness of the godhead was pleased to dwell." In other words, deity has been fully revealed in Jesus our adorable Lord. This is the "mystery of godliness" (1 Timothy 3:16).

The gnostics used the term "the fullness" *(pleroma)* for the divine essence dwelling in unapproachable light, and in a lesser sense for the illumination that comes when one reaches the higher plane of knowledge. But all the divine *pleroma* dwelt in Jesus. All that God is, He is; so we may now say, "We know God in knowing Him." Jesus has fully revealed God.

As we ponder the wondrous truths in Colossians 1:15-19, we will feel more and more that the mysteries we have here are beyond the ability of the human mind to grasp. Here is truth for pious meditation that will stir the soul to worship and offer thanksgiving; this truth is not at all for the exercise of the intellect in theological speculations. As we read we want to bow our hearts in lowly adoration and gaze on the face of Him who has come from the glory that He had with the Father throughout eternity so that we can know God.

Christ the Sacrifice (Colossians 1:20-22)

In verses 15-19 Christ is presented as the "firstborn of every creature" and the "firstborn from the dead." In these two distinct presentations we see His twofold headship: first we see His headship over all creation and then we see Him as Head of the body, the church. In verses 20-22 two aspects of reconciliation are presented: first the future reconciliation of "all things"; and then the present reconciliation of individuals. For both the universe and the individual sinner, He in whom all the fullness of the godhead dwells has "made peace through the blood of his cross" (Colossians 1:20).

Colossians 1:21 depicts man as alienated and an enemy, with his wicked works making his hostility obvious. Since sin has come between God and man, expiation is required before the guilty rebel can be received by God in peace, but in Scripture man is never called on to make his own peace with God.

Sin has lifted up its serpent head not only on earth, but also in Heaven. In fact sin began in Heaven when Lucifer apostatized, taking with him a vast number of the angelic hosts. Therefore the heavens themselves were unclean in the sight of God and needed to be purified by a better sacrifice than those offered under the law.

On the cross Christ tasted death and so far-reaching are the results of His work that eventually "all things" on earth and in Heaven will be reconciled to God on the basis of what He accomplished there. So peace has been made by Christ's sacrifice.

In spite of that fact, rebels remain. They are like guerrilla bands who insist on fighting after their nations' leaders have agreed on terms of peace. So while "Jesus' blood, through earth and skies, / Mercy, free boundless mercy, cries," men and demons persist in refusing to acknowledge the divine authority.

For the angels who rebelled, the terms of peace offer no pardon, but to the sinful sons of Adam clemency is extended, and he who will may trust in Christ and thus be reconciled to God. "Being justified by faith, we have peace with God through our Lord Jesus Christ" (Romans 5:1).

The reconciliation of "all things" includes two spheres: earth and Heaven (Colossians 1:20). The time will come when all in earth and all in Heaven will be happily reconciled to God.

Where subjugation rather than reconciliation is in view, there are three spheres, as in Philippians 2:10: Heaven, earth, and "under the earth." Heavenly, earthly, and infernal beings will at last recognize the authority of our Lord Jesus Christ, but Scripture does not hold out any hope that the sad inhabitants of the infernal regions will ever be reconciled to God.

Colossians 1:20 carries us on to the new Heaven and the new earth where righteousness will dwell, where the tabernacle of God will be with men (Revelation 21:3), and where all the redeemed and elect angels will abide with Him in holy harmony. Sin ruptured the state of peace and harmony that once existed between God and His creatures, but Christ in death has wrought reconciliation, making it possible for that lost concord to be re-established in a new creation.

This reconciliation is already accomplished for individual sinners who "were sometime alienated and enemies" (Colossians 1:21), but through grace have been reconciled to God by the death of His Son. The cross demonstrated the infinite love of the offended deity and when by faith the soul comprehends that love, the enmity is destroyed. The affections of the renewed man are drawn out to God revealed in Christ. Motivated by God's love, the apostle exclaimed:

> All things are of God, who hath reconciled us to himself by Jesus Christ, and hath given to us the ministry of reconciliation; To wit, that God was in Christ, reconciling the world unto himself, not imputing their trespasses unto them; and hath committed unto us the word of reconciliation. Now then we are ambassadors for Christ, as though God did beseech you by us: we pray you in Christ's stead, be ye reconciled to God (2 Corinthians 5:18-20).

It is not the holy, wondrous life of Christ that has reconciled us to God. It is His sacrificial death. And as a result of that death we will eventually be presented to the Father and we will be "unblameable and unreproveable in his sight" (Colossians 1:22).

The sentence begun in verse 21 is not concluded in verse 22, but verse 23 introduces a new subject, which must be considered separately.

Paul's Ministry (Colossians 1:23-25)

Verse 23 begins, "If ye continue in the faith..." The first word "if" has perplexed timid souls who hardly dare to accept the truth of the Christian's eternal security because they are so conscious of their own weakness and insufficiency. But when Paul's words are rightly understood, there is nothing in them to disturb any sincere believer in the Lord Jesus Christ. There are a number of similar *ifs* in the New Testament, and all are used when the writer wanted to test the reality of his readers' profession of faith.

For example in 1 Corinthians 15:1-2 we read, "Brethren, I declare unto you the gospel which I preached unto you, which also ye have received, and wherein ye stand; By which also ye are saved, *if* ye keep in memory what I preached unto you, unless ye have believed in vain" (italics added). Here the "if" was inserted to trouble the consciences of any who, having professed to believe the gospel, were in danger of forgetting the message because they had never really received the truth into their hearts. Paul wanted them to examine carefully the basis of their profession of faith. Many people readily profess to adopt Christianity and unite themselves outwardly with the church although they have never truly turned to the Lord in repentance and found rest for their souls through confidence in His finished work. Such endure for a time, but soon forget the claims of the gospel when Satanic allurements draw them away.

We find a similar "if" in Hebrews 3:6: "But Christ as a son over his own house; whose house are we, *if* we hold fast the confidence and the rejoicing of the hope firm unto the end" (italics added). The meaning is plain. It is not enough to profess to have the Christian hope. Those who are truly saved will "hold fast...unto the end" (also see Hebrews 10:38-39). Endurance is the proof of reality. What God implants in the soul is lasting and we may be assured "that he which hath begun a good work in [anyone] will perform it until the day of Jesus Christ" (Philippians 1:6), at which time He will come for His ransomed people and complete in glory what His grace began on earth.

Paul did not pretend to know who of the Colossians were really born of God. While he had confidence that most of them were, he wanted to stir up the consciences of any who were becoming slack. Their readiness to adopt new and fanciful systems was a cause for grave concern. Those who are really children of God, grounded and strengthened in the truth, will not be moved away from the hope of the gospel. Knowing what it has already done for them, they will not lightly turn away from it to some new and untried theory.

The Colossians had heard this gospel as in the providence of God it had been "preached to every creature which is under heaven"

(Colossians 1:23). A better translation would probably be "preached in all the creation under Heaven." It is hardly thinkable that the apostle meant that every creature in the habitable earth had heard the gospel. But it is a wonderful testimony to the devotion of the early believers that within one generation after our Lord's ascension, the evangel had been carried throughout the known world. Referring to this gospel, the apostle wrote, "Whereof I Paul am made a minister." The indefinite article lends plausibility to the idea that the ministry is a special class to which all believers do not belong, but the apostle was not claiming that he was a minister in the sense in which that term has been used in later years. He meant that he was addicted to the work of the ministry; he said in Romans 1:9, "I serve [God] with my spirit in the gospel of his Son." This gospel ministry has been committed by God not only to Paul, but to all believers. Paul shared with others the task of making the testimony known, but it was given to him to reveal it in a most excellent way. As preached by Paul, the message bore the distinctive character of "the gospel of the glory" (as "the glorious gospel" of 2 Corinthians 4:4 is sometimes translated).

Another ministry had been given to Paul: he was also to serve the body of Christ. He was to provide godly shepherd-care, enduring affliction for the blessing of Christ's beautiful flock. So he rejoiced in whatever he was called on to suffer on behalf of the people of God.

Christ suffered "once for all" on the cross "to put away sin" (Hebrews 10:10; 9:26) and His faithful servants suffer in fellowship with Him for the perfecting of the saints—that is, they "fill up that which is behind [lacking] of the afflictions of Christ...for his body's sake, which is the church" (Colossians 1:24). The people of the Lord are precious to every real servant of God and he realizes that in serving them and enduring trials on their behalf he is ministering in place of his absent Lord. The more devoted he is to Christ's interests down here during His absence, the more he will face this kind of suffering.

In Colossians 1:25 Paul, speaking of the church, said, "Whereof I am made a minister, according to the dispensation of God which is given to me for you, to fulfil the word of God." Note that the

Greek word that is translated "dispensation" here can also be rendered "stewardship." God made Paul a steward of "the mystery" mentioned in 1:26.

Paul's God-given ministry to the church was to complete the divine testimony, or to fill up the Word of God, for the whole counsel of God was not made known until Paul received his revelation of "the mystery." It was a special revelation given not to the twelve, but to him as the apostle of the new dispensation. This mystery he unfolded more fully elsewhere, noticeably in the Epistle to the Ephesians, which is the correlative of the Epistle to the Colossians.

The Mystery (Colossians 1:26-29)

As we continue to read about the mystery revealed to Paul, we need to remember that the mysteries of the New Testament are not necessarily things mysterious or abstruse. Rather, they are sacred secrets made known to the initiated. These divine secrets could never have been discovered either by human reason or even by a child of God unless a special revelation had been given to him. The gnostics made much of the mysteries of their systems, but the Christian mysteries are in vivid contrast to these dreams of insubordinate men.

The mystery of the church as the body of Christ was never made known either in Old Testament times or in the days when our Lord was on the earth. We are told distinctly that the mystery "hath been hid from ages and from generations, but now is made manifest to his saints" (Colossians 1:26). The divine method of making it known was to give a special revelation to the apostle Paul, as he told us in Ephesians 3:3. But this revelation was not for him only. The ministry committed to him was to pass the revelation on to the saints.

Colossians 1:27 tells us that to these saints "God would make known what is the riches of the glory of this mystery among the Gentiles; which is Christ in you, the hope of glory." I have quoted the King James version, but the verse can also be translated as follows: "God did make known the wealth of the splendor of this sacred secret among the nations, which is Christ among the Gentiles, the hope of glory." The Old Testament Scriptures clearly predicted the calling of the Gentiles, but always with the thought that they would be in subjection to Israel. During the present dispensation Israel has been set aside because of unbelief (Romans 11) and Christ is working among the nations to attract weary hearts to Himself without any thought of Jewish priority. Believing Jews and Gentiles are united by the Holy Spirit's baptism into one body, and thus all distinctions are eliminated; the middle wall of partition is broken down. This is the mystery of the church as the body of Christ.

Christ Himself, the Head of this body, was the apostle's theme. Note his words at the beginning of Colossians 1:28: "Whom we preach." To substitute "what" for "whom" here would be a serious mistake. Christianity is centered in a person and no one preaches the gospel who does not preach Christ. When there is faith in Him, the Spirit unites the believer to Him.

How earnest was the apostle, "warning every man" and seeking to lead Christians into the knowledge of this precious truth! His was the true pastor's heart, and with this he combined in a marvelous way the teacher's gift. The subject of his ministry was "the perfecting of the saints" (Ephesians 4:12) and his desire was that every man should be complete or full-grown in Christ Jesus. To this end he labored as divine energy worked powerfully in him for the salvation of souls and the upbuilding of the people of God.

False teachers want to turn the eyes of the saints away from Christ, the glorified Head of the body, and toward specious systems of Satanic origin. Thus they would "draw away disciples after them," as Paul warned the Ephesian elders (Acts 20:30). But all true Spirit-given ministry is christocentric. Every faithful minister of the new dispensation wants to lift up the Lord Jesus before the admiring gaze of His people so that, looking on Him, they will be transfigured into His likeness. Like John the Baptist, the true teacher says, "He must increase, but I must decrease" (John 3:30).

No man can preach the whole truth today unless he enters into the twofold ministry of the gospel and the church. He needs to proclaim the gospel to sinners, "for it is the power of God unto salvation to every one that believeth" (Romans 1:16). And he needs to minister to the church by teaching the saints their present privileges and corresponding responsibilities and by building them up in the faith. He is called not only to win sinners to Christ so that they may be saved from impending wrath, but also to make good churchmen out of those already saved.

I do not mean that the preacher should insist on what is called denominational loyalty or that he should endeavor to sectionalize the saints and bring them into bondage to legal principles and practices for which there is no Biblical basis. His calling is to show the saints that in the new creation they are linked with their risen, glorified Head, and to help them recognize the unity of the body in which all believers have a part. Thus as they walk together in the bond of peace, they may endeavor to keep the unity formed by the Holy Spirit.

Sad indeed are the divisions among men of "like precious faith" (2 Peter 1:1). The unity of the body is often disturbed by men of sectarian spirit and narrow cramped sympathies who are more concerned about building up local causes than edifying the body of Christ. It is perfectly true that the saints are not to neglect local responsibilities, but they should not disregard the unity that the Holy Spirit has created. "The unity of the Spirit" (Ephesians 4:3) is not a confederacy of assemblies of Christians, but the abiding unity that the Holy Ghost has formed by baptizing believers into one body. I fail to keep this unity if I set at nought any fellow believer. As "members one of another" having "the same care one for another," we show in a practical way the truth that we are one in Christ (Romans 12:5; 1 Corinthians 12:25).

CHAPTER TWO
CHRIST, THE TRUE WISDOM

The Mystery of God (Colossians 2:1-7)

Men who know little of the deep convictions that stirred the heart of the apostle Paul will have difficulty realizing the intensity of his feelings when the truth of God was questioned and the people of the Lord were in danger of being corrupted by false doctrine and turned aside from the simplicity that is in Christ. He wrote to the Colossians, "I would that ye knew what great conflict I have for you" (2:1). This verse could also be translated, "I would have you know what intense agony I have for you."

Paul was not one who could play fast and loose with revealed truth. His very soul was tortured when Christ was dishonored by those who professed His name. He was not a self-complacent liberal theologian, carelessly tolerant of any teaching, no matter how pernicious, as long as it did not disrupt outward unity.

The apostle was intensely concerned about the fact that at both Colossae and Laodicea, designing men were seeking to seduce the saints from their first love—that is, Christ. We know that the enemy was largely successful at Laodicea, for the glorified Son of man charged the Laodiceans with being "neither cold nor hot" (Revelation 3:15). Proud of their culture and wealth, they were indifferent to Christ. Paul sought to save the Laodiceans and Colossians from such indifference, and it is to be hoped that he succeeded with the Colossians.

Truth unites. Error divides. Paul wanted the hearts of the Colossians to be "knit together in love" as they understood "the

47

mystery of God" (Colossians 2:2). There is some manuscript diversity in the wording of the last part of this verse. The King James version reads, "The mystery of God, and of the Father, and of Christ"; this translation is admittedly peculiar. A more understandable rendering of the same manuscript would be "The mystery of God, even of the Father, and of Christ." But Paul's meaning seems clearer in other manuscripts that can be translated, "The mystery of God, even Christ"; this version is probably the correct one. Paul was referring to the great divine mystery of the "new man" (Ephesians 2:15). As we read in 1 Corinthians 12:12-13:

> As the body is one, and hath many members, and all the members of that one body, being many, are one body: so also is Christ. For by one Spirit are we all baptized into one body, whether we be Jews or Gentiles, whether we be bond or free; and have been all made to drink into one Spirit.

There probably should be a definite article before "Christ" in 1 Corinthians 12:12, for it is the mystical Christ that is in view. I take it that we have a similar idea in Colossians 2:2. "The mystery of God" is that which He has now revealed regarding Christ as Head of the body and consequently of the entire new creation.

As believers comprehend "the mystery," they are delivered from vain speculations and fleshly strivings, for all perfection is found in Christ. The apostle wanted the Colossians to have "the full assurance of understanding" as their hearts acknowledged the wealth of this great mystery. In Hebrews 6:11 we read of "the full assurance of hope" and in Hebrews 10:22 we read of the "full assurance of faith." Full assurance of understanding, hope, and faith—these together establish the soul and set it free from doubt and fear.

In Christ—or, if you prefer, in this mystery of God now revealed—"are hid all the treasures of wisdom and knowledge" (Colossians 2:3). It is not necessary to go elsewhere—that is, to investigate human systems and philosophies—to find an explanation of the mystery of the universe and the relationship of the Creator to His creatures. As we learn to know Christ better and understand the truth concerning Him, every question is answered, every perplexity made clear, and every doubt dissolved. Why turn aside to idle speculations, no matter how pretentious, when God has spoken in His Son and given His holy Word to lead us by the Spirit into all truth? Paul wanted to protect the saints from being led astray by persuasive talk or "with enticing words" (Colossians 2:4). Advocates of error delight to clothe their evil systems in most attractive phraseology in an attempt to entrap the souls of the unwary. Only the truth of God can preserve believers when they are exposed to such deception. It is important to remember that no amount of intellectual culture or human learning can take the place of divine revelation. If God has not spoken, we may speculate and reason as we please. But if He has given the truth in His Word, there is an end to all our theorizing. In Colossians 2 Paul showed how Christ is the antidote for human philosophy, Jewish legality, oriental mysticism, and carnal asceticism. These have no place in Christianity. Christ supersedes them all.

The apostle knew (through the report of Epaphras) what Christ had meant to the Colossian saints from the time of their conversion and he was concerned that they might now be turned aside from Him. Though not with them physically, he was one with them in spirit and he rejoiced in all he heard of their godly orderliness and steadfast confidence in Christ. They had begun their Christian journey in faith; moreover they had continued in the same paths of truth and Paul did not want them to go astray. They had received Christ Jesus the Lord—that is, they had trusted Him as Savior and owned Him as Master—and the apostle now wanted them to walk in Him, not turning aside to any new system or perversion of the truth.

Paul's desire was that they be "rooted and built up" in Christ (Colossians 2:7). Then, as a tree sends its roots deep down into the soil, they would draw on hidden sources of supply, all centered in Christ; and as a building founded on a rock is firmly established, they would recognize Christ as their only foundation. The apostle used the same figures of speech in Ephesians 3:17: "That Christ may dwell in your hearts by faith; that ye, being rooted and grounded in love." God is love; so to be rooted and established in love is to be rooted in and founded on God, God revealed in Christ.

If a man walks "in him" (Colossians 2:6), he is established in the faith, "abounding therein with thanksgiving" (2:7). Nothing causes the soul to overflow with worship and gratitude to God so much as a deep knowledge of Christ. True joy is only found in acquaintance with Him. Why then should anyone go after speculative theories that cannot give the soul peace and that make light of Christ the Head?

Every system that makes light of Christ or His atoning blood is from the pit and is to be shunned as a viper by all who know Him. So-called Christian Science is an example. A follower of Mrs. Eddy, the now-deceased head of the cult, visited a simple Christian woman and labored long to explain the professed benefits and beauties of that system. After listening for several hours, the Christian found herself utterly unable to follow the specious sophistries and vapid theorizings of her visitor. Finally the Christian exclaimed, "I do not understand what you are getting at. Can't you put it all in simpler terms so that I may know what it is that you want me to believe?"

"Well," replied the cultist, "in the first place you must understand this: God is a principle not a person. You see, my dear, we worship a principle."

"Enough," exclaimed the other with a relieved expression on her countenance, "That would never do for me! I worship a personal God revealed in Christ, my blessed, adorable Savior." And at once her soul was delivered from the net spread before her by the soft-voiced emissary of Satan who had been endeavoring to ensnare her.

The test of any system is whether it makes light of Christ.

"What think ye of Christ?" is the test,
　　　To try both your state and your scheme;
You cannot be right in the rest,
　　　Unless you think rightly of Him:
As Jesus appears in your view—
　　　As He is beloved or not,
So God is disposed to you,
　　　And mercy or wrath is your lot.

Some take Him a creature to be—
    A man, or an angel at most;
But they have not feelings like me,
    Nor know themselves wretched and lost.
So guilty, so helpless am I,
    I durst not confide in His blood,
Nor on His protection rely,
    Unless I were sure He is God.

Some call Him a Saviour, in word,
    But mix their own works with His plan;
And hope He His help will afford,
    When they have done all that they can:
If doings prove rather too light
    (A little they own they may fail),
They purpose to make up full weight,
    By casting His name in the scale.

Some style Him "the Pearl of great price,"
    And say, He's the fountain of joys;
Yet feed upon folly and vice,
    And cleave to the world and its toys.
Like Judas, the Saviour they kiss,
    And while they salute Him, betray:
Oh! what will profession like this
    Avail in His terrible day?

If asked what of Jesus *I* think,
    Though still my best thoughts are but poor,
I say, He's my meat and my drink,
    My life, and my strength, and my store;
My Shepherd, my trust, and my Friend,
    My Saviour from sin and from thrall;
My Hope from beginning to end,
    My Portion, my Lord and my All.
                                    (John Newton)

The natural man cannot understand why Christians should insist on a clear-cut confession of the truth about Christ. "What does it matter," he asks, "whether Jesus is a mere man, more spiritual than most, or the divine eternal Son in the form of man? If He is only a man, He is still the great example and the master teacher. If He is more than man, He is only the revelation of the Father: by His life of love and purity He has shown us God's attitude toward all mankind and has lead us into a better understanding of God and our relationship to Him."

The natural man does not understand Scriptural truth concerning Christ. His holy life—whether only human or divinely human—can never take away our sins or fit us to stand uncondemned before the eternal throne. He had to be both God and man in order to make atonement for sin; as perfect man He had to meet every claim that the outraged deity had against sinful man. If you detract from the person of Christ, you detract from His work. If that work was not divinely perfect, there remains no other sacrifice for sins and we are left without a Savior.

But we can thank God that He who came forth from the Father has glorified Him on the earth and having finished the work that was given to Him to do, He has gone back to the glory that He had with the Father before the world was (John 16:28; 17:4-5). There He sits on the right hand of the Majesty in the heavens; the exalted man who purged our sins ever lives to make intercession for those His grace has saved (Hebrews 1:3; 7:25). Happy in this knowledge, we may well sing with chastened joy:

> Head of the Church! Thou sittest there,
> Thy members all the blessings share—
> Thy blessing, Lord, is ours:
> Our life Thou art—Thy grace sustains,
> Thy strength in us each vict'ry gains
> O'er sin and Satan's pow'rs.

May we prove our loyalty to Him, not only by confessing a true Christ with our lips, but also by giving Him the supreme place in our lives!

Human Philosophy (Colossians 2:8-10)

Nowhere in Scripture is the acquisition of knowledge condemned. It is the wisdom of this world, not its knowledge, that is foolishness with God (1 Corinthians 3:19). Philosophy is merely worldly wisdom. It is the effort of the human mind to solve the mystery of the universe, but it is not an exact science, for philosophers have never been able to come to any satisfactory conclusion about the "why" or "wherefore" of things. "The Greeks seek after wisdom," we are told in 1 Corinthians 1:22, and it was they who led the way in philosophical theorizing.

Before the divine revelation came, it was proper for man to seek by wisdom to solve the riddles that nature was constantly posing. But now that God has spoken, this is no longer necessary and it may lead to grave infidelity. From Plato to Kant, and from Kant to the last of the modern philosophers, one system of thought has overturned another; the history of philosophy is a record of contradictory, discarded hypotheses. I am not saying that the philosophers were or are dishonest men, but I am saying that many of them have failed to avail themselves of that which would unravel every knot and solve every problem: namely, the revelation of God in Christ as given in the Holy Scriptures.

Plato yearned for a divine word, *logos,* that would come with authority and make everything plain. We know that the Word is Christ, of whom John wrote: "In the beginning was the Word, and the Word was with God, and the Word was God....And the Word was made flesh, and dwelt among us, (and we beheld his glory, the glory as of the only begotten of the Father,) full of grace and truth" (John 1:1,14). The Word is no longer hidden; we do not need to search for it. Paul said in Romans 10:8-9, "The word is nigh thee, even in thy mouth, and in thy heart: that is, the word of faith, which we preach; That if thou shalt confess with thy mouth the Lord Jesus, and shalt believe in thine heart that God hath raised him from the dead, thou shalt be saved."

Socrates, pondering the "unsolvable" problems relating to possible future rewards and punishments, said, "It may be, Plato, that the Deity can forgive sins, but I do not see how." No such perplexities need trouble any honest mind now, for what philosophy could not explain, the gospel has made clear—that gospel in which the righteousness of God is revealed to sinful men. Apart from this divine revelation, the wisest philosopher of the twentieth century knows no more about the origin and destiny of man than the Athenian philosophers knew so long ago.

Two great philosophical systems were contending for mastery over the minds of men in the western world when Paul wrote his letter to the Colossians: stoicism and epicureanism. Stoicism said: "Live nobly and death cannot matter. Hold appetite in check. Become indifferent to changing conditions. Be not uplifted by good fortune nor cast down by adversity. The man is more than his circumstances; the soul is greater than the universe." Epicureanism said: "All is uncertain. We know not whence we came; we know not whither we go; we only know that after a brief life we disappear from this scene, and it is vain to deny ourselves any present joy in view of possible future ill. Let us eat and drink, for tomorrow we die."

Christianity had nothing in common with epicureanism. But the Christian message appealed to many stoics; we only need to read 1 Corinthians 9:24-27 or Philippians 4:11-13 to understand why. While the stoic might find the fulfillment of his heart's yearning in Christianity, there was nothing in stoicism that the Christian needed, for everything that was best in that system he already had in Christ.

Besides these two outstanding philosophical schools there were among both the Greeks and Romans many lesser systems, all of which sought to draw away disciples to themselves. The gnostics included parts of all the different schools of thought in their new system. From the weird guesses embodied in the pythagorean fables down to the evolutionary theories of the present time, the church of God is in conflict with all vagrant philosophies.

Against such the Christian is warned. Colossians 2:8 says, "Beware lest any man spoil [make a prey of] you through philosophy and vain deceit." Worldly philosophies may make a great show of learning, and their adherents may look down with contempt from their heights of fancied superiority on people simple enough to believe the gospel and to accept the Holy Scriptures as the inspired

Word of the living God. But in spite of all their pretentiousness, these philosophies are simply the traditions of man, "the rudiments [first principles] of the world."

The apostle expressed his contempt for mere reasoning in comparison with divine revelation. He said that the systems that claimed so much were after all but elementary; they offered the ABCs of the world to those who were in the school of Christ and who had left the kindergarten of human tradition far behind. Can a man "by searching find out God?" (Job 11:7) Impossible. But God is already known in His Son.

It is most important that Christians should heed Paul's warning in Colossians 2:8, particularly the young men who are called of God to be ministers of His Word. In the average theological seminary, far more time is given to studying philosophy than to searching the Scriptures. What a sad commentary on conditions in Christendom! A minister of an orthodox church said, "I could have graduated with honors from my seminary without ever opening the English Bible." Thank God, this is not true of all such training schools, but it is true of perhaps the majority. The result is that among the thousands of so-called ministers of Christ, many are unconverted and others who are children of God have been stunted and hindered by their philosophical education. They are utterly unable to open up the Scriptures to others, for they are ignorant of the Word themselves. Like the Bible, Christianity owes no debt to Greek, Roman, medieval, or modern philosophy.

> A glory gilds the sacred page,
> Majestic like the sun,
> It gives a light to ev'ry age;
> It gives, but borrows none.
> (William Cowper)

A man can be a well-equipped minister of Jesus Christ even if he has never heard the names of the great philosophers, pagan or Christian, and is utterly ignorant of their systems and hypotheses, provided that he will "study to shew [himself] approved unto God, a workman that needeth not to be ashamed, rightly dividing the word of truth" (2 Timothy 2:15). The truest culture, intellectual or spiritual, is that which is drawn from the constant study of the Bible. Often I come in contact with men of gracious personality, gentlemanly appearance, high spirituality, and well-trained intellect and find upon inquiry that they, like John Wesley, are "men of one book" and in some instances hardly conversant with the literature of earth.

In saying this I do not mean to put a premium on ignorance, for the knowledge of this world is not under a ban. The Christian may well avail himself of any legitimate means of becoming better acquainted with the facts of history, the findings of science, and the beauties of general literature; but let him never put human philosophy in the place of divine revelation. If he studies philosophy at all—and there is no reason why he should not do so—let him remember that God has spoken in His Son and that in the Holy Scriptures He has given us the last word on every question that philosophy raises. Robert Browning was right when he wrote:

I say, the acknowledgment of God in Christ
Accepted by thy reason, solves for thee
All questions in the earth and out of it,
And has so far advanced thee to be wise.

When the Savior revealed Himself to the Samaritan woman, she found her every question answered as she gazed on His face.

Colossians 2:9 tells us that in Christ "dwelleth all the fulness of the Godhead bodily." The word translated "fulness," *pleroma,* was a favorite term of the gnostics. It represented to them the sum of the qualities of deity, and they considered Christ to be one of many steppingstones or intermediaries leading up to the *pleroma.* But in Scripture we learn that not only are all the attributes of God seen in Christ (as Arius afterward thought and as theistic philosophers everywhere admit); the very essence of the nature of God in all its entirety dwells in Him.

All that God is, is fully revealed in Christ. He could say, "He that hath seen me hath seen the Father" (John 14:9). Therefore, if anyone asks us to describe the character of God, we can say without hesitation that God is exactly like Jesus. Jesus is the Christ, and in

Christ all the fullness of deity dwells in a body. When at last we come into the presence of the Father, we will find in Him One known and loved before, not a stranger still unknown and possibly unknowable. As J. N. Darby wrote:

> There no stranger-God shall meet thee!
> Stranger thou in courts above:
> He, who to His rest shall greet thee,
> Greets thee with a well-known love.

God is revealed; He is no longer hidden. All His glory shines in the face of Christ Jesus. And for me as a believer the mystery of the universe is solved.

> And that which seemed to me before
> One wild, confused Babel,
> Is now a fire-tongued Pentecost
> Proclaiming Christ is able;
> And all creation its evangel
> Utters forth abroad
> Into mine ears since once I know
> My Saviour Christ is God.

In Colossians 2:10 we are told, "And ye are complete in him." In Christ dwells all the *pleroma* of deity, and we have our *pleroma* in Him. We do not need to go elsewhere for illumination or information. "Of his fullness have all we received, and grace for grace. For the law was given by Moses, but grace and truth came by Jesus Christ. No man hath seen God at any time; the only begotten Son, which is in the bosom of the Father, he hath declared him" (John 1:16-18). This revelation floods our being with rapture, fills our cup of joy, and satisfies every demand of the intellect. We are filled full in Him.

In Ephesians 1:6 we are told that we are "accepted in the beloved." In that sense—in our standing as believers—we may be said to be complete in Him. But in Colossians 2:10 our state rather than our standing is in view—the state of those who have found every need met in Christ, "which is the head of all principality and power."

Principalities and *powers* are terms relating to different ranks of spiritual beings. The gnostics reveled in a pretended knowledge of the nature and function of these glorious intelligences and placed them high above Christ. According to them, Christ was merely the one who introduced the initiate into the fellowship of this serried host that lead up to the invisible God. But the truth is just the opposite, for all principalities and powers—and these may be good or evil, fallen or unfallen—were created by Him and for Him in whom all the fullness dwells (Colossians 1:16; 2:9). He is the Head of all angelic companies as well as all human beings. "No place too high for Him is found, / No place too high in Heaven." God wants His people to realize that He who stooped to the depths of the shame and suffering of the cross for their salvation, is God over all "blessed for ever" (Romans 9:5).

Observe that it is immediately after the declaration of Christ's headship over all angels (Colossians 2:10) that we are told of the depths of His humiliation, for God would never separate the person and the work of our Lord Jesus. God would have us remember that it was because of Christ's transcendent character and His true deity that He could undertake the work of purging our sins by giving Himself as a sacrifice on our behalf. He had to be who He was in order to do what He did.

The sin question could never have been settled by a created being, for the issues were too great. A free translation of Psalm 49:7-8 says of all men: "None of them can by any means redeem his brother or give to God a ransom for him, for the redemption of the soul costs too much. Therefore, let it alone forever." These verses from the Psalms emphasize what Paul had in mind when he wrote to the Colossians: Low thoughts of Christ result from low thoughts of sin. When a person realizes the enormity of his iniquity, he knows that only the Daysman for whom Job yearned can save him from such a load of guilt. Christ, because He is God and man, can "lay his hand upon us both" (Job 9:33) and thus, by making atonement for sin, bring God and man together in holy, happy harmony.

Can a mere man do this?
Yet Christ saith, this He lived and died to do.
Call Christ, then, the illimitable God,
Or lost!

(Robert Browning)

To all the questionings of the mind of man about spiritual verities, God has no other answer than Christ; and no other is needed,
for Christ is the answer to them all. He who refuses Christ refuses
God's last word to mankind. He has said everything He has to say
in sending Him into the world as the giver of life and the propitia-
tion for our sins. To turn from Him is to refuse the living incarnation of the Truth and to block out everything but error and delusion.

Jewish Legalism (Colossians 2:11-17)

This somewhat lengthy passage begins in the middle of a sentence. Verse 11, though part of the sentence begun in verse 10, introduces a new subject and that subject is legalism. While philosophy
is the result of the human mind working independently of divine
revelation, legalism is the result of the attempt to use a divinely
given code (to which precepts of men may have been added) as a
means of salvation or as a means of growth in grace. Legalism is
not Scriptural. Galatians 2:16 forever rules out legal works as a
means of procuring salvation: "By the works of the law shall no
flesh be justified." Just as effectually, Romans 6:14 forbids the
thought that holiness of life for the Christian is found in subjecting
himself to legal principles: "Ye are not under the law, but under
grace." We are told in 1 Corinthians 15:56 that the law is "the strength
of sin." The law is not, as multitudes have supposed, the strength of
holiness or the power for righteousness. The dynamic of spirituality is the indwelling Holy Spirit, who points us to Christ crucified,
raised, and glorified.

Gnosticism was as much indebted to legalistic Judaism, which it
perverted to its own ends, and to a weird Jewish cabbalism as it was
to the insipid reasonings of Gentile philosophers and Mithraic and

Zoroastrian mysticism. In Colossians 2:11-17 the apostle dealt specifically with Jewish legalism and showed how Christians have been forever delivered from the law. They are now linked with the risen Christ and for them to go back to the law to perfect themselves in holiness would be to fall from grace (as Paul showed in the Epistle to the Galatians). Legalists virtually set aside the gospel of grace; they forget that having begun in the Spirit we are not to be made perfect by the flesh.

Ever dogging the footsteps of the great apostle to the Gentiles were those who sought to pervert his converts by teaching them that they had "to keep the law of Moses." These legalists said, "Except ye be circumcised after the manner of Moses, ye cannot be saved" (Acts 15:1,5). Although the council at Jerusalem gave forth no uncertain sound in opposition to this teaching, the decisions of the council were by no means everywhere accepted. It was hard for converts from Judaism to realize their complete deliverance from the law of Moses as a rule of life and from the ceremonies and rituals of that law as a means of growth in grace.

Through the inspiration of the Holy Spirit, Paul handled the issue in a remarkable manner. Having declared that we have our completeness in Christ, our exalted Head, he continued: "In whom also ye are circumcised with the circumcision made without hands, in putting off the body of the sins of the flesh by the circumcision of Christ" (Colossians 2:11). The words "of the sins" were probably not in the original manuscript and could be omitted. It is not merely the sins of the flesh, but the flesh itself that is in view here.

Circumcision is the cutting off of the flesh physically, and the ritual was given by God to picture the complete setting aside of the carnal nature. This is what God has done in the cross of Christ. It was the end of the flesh as viewed from the divine standpoint; Christ was cut off by death as He stood vicariously in our place.

In the circumcision "made without hands" the carnal nature is cut off, put to one side as absolutely worthless. "The flesh," we read, "profiteth nothing" (John 6:63). "It is not subject to the law of God, neither indeed can be" (Romans 8:7). Therefore God makes no attempt to improve the flesh; consequently there is no place for claims to merit as far as man is concerned. He has none and, praise God, he needs none. All merit is in Another!

The same truth is demonstrated in Christian baptism. Personally I have no sympathy for those who in our day would like to do away with water baptism; they argue that there is now only one baptism—that is, the baptism of the Holy Spirit. Ephesians 4:4-6, which refers to water baptism, has been true ever since Pentecost.

The book of Ephesians, one of the prison Epistles, does proclaim the truth revealed to Paul about the church as the body of Christ, but he did not receive the revelation of this mystery *after* he went to prison. He made this mystery known throughout his ministry. In Romans 16:26 he said that this mystery had been "made known to all nations for the obedience of faith." The rapture, which is part of this mystery, is taught in his earliest Epistle, First Thessalonians. When he said to the Ephesian elders, "I have not shunned to declare unto you all the counsel of God" (Acts 20:27), that counsel in its entirety had already been made known to him and proclaimed among the Gentiles.

The baptism of the Holy Spirit whereby believers were brought into the body of Christ took place on the day of Pentecost. By this baptism the body, the church, was formed. There is no hint in Scripture that any such supernatural work was widespread after Paul's imprisonment. When Paul wrote to the Ephesians, the body had been formed for years, and each believer was added to it when that believer received the Spirit.

In my judgment Ephesians 4:5 cannot refer to Pentecost because this event is already mentioned in the previous verse. Verse 4 refers to the full revelation of the mystery: the body formed by the Spirit's baptism and waiting for the coming of the Lord. We read, "There is one body, and one Spirit...and one hope of your calling."

Then in verse 5 we read of "one Lord, one faith, one baptism." This refers to responsibility here on earth: Christ is to be acknowledged as Lord; the church is to "contend for the faith which was once delivered unto the saints" (Jude 3); and water baptism in the name of the Father, Son, and Holy Spirit is to be observed in recognition of our subjection to the one Lord. In Ephesians 4:5 Paul was not citing a formula or making a list; he was declaring the broad fact that Christianity knows only one baptism, and that of course is baptism unto the death of Jesus Christ. To speak of the Holy Spirit's baptism as a burial with Christ is nonsense. It is after my identification by faith with the death, burial, and resurrection of Christ that the Holy Spirit baptizes me into the body.

I am not saying that people who for various reasons, valid or otherwise, have not been scripturally baptized are not in Christ. In drawing an illustration from what is scripturally correct, one does not unchristianize those who fall short either because of ignorance or willfulness.

The argument of Colossians 2:12, as I see it, is this: The Christian confesses his identification with a rejected Christ in his baptism. He admits that he as a natural man deserved to die, and he has died in Christ's death. With the death of the natural man comes the end of the legalistic man and therefore the end of all self-effort, of every attempt to improve the flesh by subjecting it to ordinances or regulations, whether divinely given as in the Old Testament or humanly devised as in so many unscriptural systems. God is not trying to improve the old man; He has judged him too evil for any improvement and has therefore set him to one side in death. Baptism is the recognition of this. It is burial unto death.

Colossians 2:12 continues, "Wherein also ye are risen with him through the faith of the operation of God, who hath raised him from the dead." The preponderance of evidence is, I believe, in favor of substituting "In whom" for "Wherein." It is through faith in the risen Christ that we become the recipients of the new life and are henceforth viewed by God as those who, having gone down into death with Him, are now one with Him in resurrection. What place does legalism have here? None whatever. To put the new man, the man in Christ, under rules and regulations is contrary to the entire principle of new creation.

This thought is further emphasized in Colossians 2:13: "You, being dead in your sins and the uncircumcision of your flesh, hath he quickened together with him, having forgiven you all trespasses." (The same word is translated "sins" in the first part of the verse and "trespasses" in the last.) Paul was saying that God has forgiven our trespasses and we who once were dead in our trespasses and as Gentiles were uncircumcised in our flesh have now been made to live together with Christ.

Colossians 2:14 continues, "Blotting out the handwriting of ordinances that was against us, which was contrary to us, and took it out of the way, nailing it to his cross." The expression "the handwriting of ordinances" could only be properly used to refer to the ten commandments, which we are distinctly told were given in the handwriting of God. The sinfulness of our natures made our disobedience to the law a foregone conclusion and therefore the law (the ten divinely given ordinances) condemned us to death. But the law has now been taken out of our way and no longer hangs over us as an unfulfilled obligation. Christ nailed the law to His cross.

We might better understand the expression "nailing it to his cross" if we remember what was customary under Roman law when a criminal was executed by crucifixion, hanging, or impalement. The law the criminal had broken or the nature of his offense was written on a placard, which was nailed above his head so that everyone would know how Rome administered vengeance on those who violated her criminal code. Pilate wrote out the inscription to be placed over the head of Christ Jesus—in Hebrew, Greek, and Latin—so that all might know why the patient sufferer from Galilee was being publicly executed. John 19:19 tells us that Pilate wrote: "Jesus of Nazareth the King of the Jews." As the people read this inscription, they understood that He was being crucified because he made Himself a King and was thus disloyal to caesar.

But as God looked on that cross His holy eye saw, as it were, another inscription altogether. He saw, nailed on the cross above the head of His blessed Son, the ten handwritten ordinances given at Sinai. It was because this law had been broken in every point that Jesus poured out His blood, thus giving His life to redeem us from the curse of the law. And so all of our sins have been paid for. At the cross the law, which we had so dishonored, was magnified to the full as Jesus Himself satisfied divine justice. Thus Christ has become the end of the law to everyone who believes (Romans 10:4). Of course when Paul spoke of the ordinances that were against "us" (Colossians 2:14), he had Jewish believers in mind, for Gentiles were not under the law. But it is true now in principle for all to whom the knowledge of the law has come. Christ has by His death met every claim against us and canceled the debt we could not pay. Now as a victorious leader He has come forth from the tomb. He made a prey of the evil principalities and powers who gloated over His apparent defeat when He was crucified, but are themselves now defeated in His resurrection. Having made a spectacle of them, He has ascended to Heaven in a glorious triumph.

> His be the Victor's name,
> Who fought the fight alone;
> Triumphant saints no honor claim,
> His conquest was their own.
>
> By weakness and defeat,
> He won a glorious crown,
> Trod all our foes beneath His feet,
> By being trodden down.
>
> . . . .
> Bless, bless the Conquer'r slain,
> Slain in His victory;
> Who lived, Who died, Who lives again,
> For thee, His church, for thee!
>
> (Whitlock Gandy)

Christ took our place on the cross and now we share in all the results of that sacrifice. We are one with Him in the new creation. The law and all its ritual was given to man in the flesh. Christians are not in the flesh, but in the Spirit, and the law as such has nothing to say to the man in this new sphere beyond the reach of death.

Paul concluded this marvelous passage with a solemn admonition not to permit ourselves to be disturbed by any who would put us back under the law in any shape or form: "Let no man therefore judge you in meat, or in drink, or in respect of an holyday, or of the new moon, or of the sabbath days" (Colossians 2:16). All these once had their place and an obedient child of the old covenant scrupulously observed the regulations regarding them. They were, however, only "a shadow of things to come [things which have now come]; but the body is of Christ" (2:17).

In the Old Testament dispensation the light of God was shining on Christ, and all the forms and ceremonies including the weekly sabbaths were but shadows cast by Him. Since He Himself has come and fulfilled all the redemptive types, the believer has everything in Jesus. The fact that Colossians 2:16 links the sabbath with the other ceremonies shows clearly that the rule of life for the believer is not the ten commandments. While acknowledging this law to be holy, just, and good, the new-creation man is not under it. He is, as Paul said in 1 Corinthians 9:21, "under the law to Christ"; that is, his responsibility now is to walk in fellowship with the risen Christ, the Head of the body of which he is but a feeble member. In him now dwells the Holy Spirit, who is the power of his new life, which is demonstrated in his subjection to the exalted Lord.

No one needs to fear that the result of being in subjection to Christ rather than being under the law as a rule of life will be a lower standard of piety. Christ's standard is far higher. The person whose one thought and desire is to display the risen life of Christ in all his ways will lead a holier life than he who is seeking to subject the flesh to rules and regulations—even though the rules were given from Heaven in a past dispensation. Evidence of this is seen in the contrast between the sabbath of the law and the Lord's day of the new creation. There is no commandment in the New Testament inculcating the sacredness of the first day of the week and demanding that Christians observe it scrupulously for holy purposes, yet the consensus of judgment of spiritually-minded believers all through the centuries has led to the honoring of this day as a time of worship, meditation, and Christian testimony. From a spiritual standpoint, therefore, the Lord's day has been given a pre-eminence that the Jewish sabbath never had.

We are not called on to substitute a Christian ritual for the Jewish ritual that we have discarded. Now we worship by the Spirit of God, who delights in directing the hearts of the redeemed toward Him to whom they owe all their blessings. Thus all that is of the flesh or carnal, being prefatory and transient, must give way to that which is spiritual and abiding.

Gnostic Mysticism (Colossians 2:18-19)

The natural man is distinctly religious. He does not need to be regenerated in order to grope for God. While it is true of all the unsaved that "there is none that seeketh after God" in the sense of seeking Him for His own sake (Romans 3:11), it has been well said that man is incurably religious; he must have something to worship. And so Satan has supplied him with cults of all descriptions to suit every type of mind.

One of the oldest religious systems is Parseeism, which has survived even to our own day. Parseeism, which is based on the Zend Avesta, is supposed to have originated with the Persian hero and prophet Zoroaster, or Zarathustra as he is called in the Persian scriptures. This system teaches a mystical dualism: Ahura Mazda, or Ormuzd, is the infinite god, the eternal light; a lesser deity Ahriman, the prince of darkness, sometimes looked on as the creator of matter, is in constant conflict with the supreme deity. According to Parseeism, Ahriman is destined to wage war against the light for twelve thousand years and then his kingdom of darkness will be destroyed.

This system permeated various schools of thought and in apostolic days had been widely accepted throughout the Greek and Roman world under the name of Mithraism. Its votaries went everywhere proclaiming it as the great unifying world religion. It was a vast secret society with initiates going from one mystical degree to another until they became experts. This Satanic system trembled before the advancing hosts of Christianity and finally sought to combine certain of its views with a part of the Christian revelation; and as we have seen, a new religion was formed by an eclectic combination of Judaism, Greek philosophy, and oriental mysticism. The new religion divided into many different sects—all unsound in their teaching about Christ, all rejecting the inspiration of the Holy Scriptures and substituting the vain speculations of the human mind.

Found in one or another of these sects were imitations of almost every Christian doctrine—with certain accretions and contradictions that made them most dangerous. Years after the apostle John died, Justin Martyr wrote, "Many spirits are abroad in the world and the credentials they display are splendid gifts of mind, eloquence and logic. Christian, look carefully, and ask for the print of the nails." All these sects denied the true Christ of God who gave Himself for our sins on the cross of shame. Some, like the docetists, taught that the humanity of Jesus was simply an appearance, unreal and immaterial. The first Epistle of John refutes this teaching in a wonderful way. Another sect, afterward headed up by Cerinthus—the great arch-heretic of the second century who was called by Polycarp "the firstborn of Satan"—taught that Jesus was the natural son of Joseph and Mary, that He died on the cross to separate Himself from His own sin, and that the Christ (identified with the eternal Spirit) came to Him at His baptism but left Him at the cross. This faction seems to have been on the mind of the apostle Paul and he combated it in a masterly manner.

In all these sects, knowledge was given pre-eminence over faith. Faith, which is confidence in revealed testimony, was repudiated by theorists who professed acquaintance with divine mysteries far beyond that of ordinary people and quite in advance of the Biblical revelation. In their pride and folly they put a great number of spirit-beings known as eons between the soul and the unknowable God. These eons were all classified and given names such as Reason, Wisdom, Power—names reflecting divine attributes. All this appeals to the natural man.

It sounds like humility to say, "In myself I am so utterly ignorant and unworthy that it is not for me to go directly to God the Father or to Christ the Son. I will therefore avail myself of mediating angels and spirits who can present my cause in a more suitable manner than I can myself." But it is really pride of intellect and the grossest unbelief, for God has declared that there is "one mediator between God and men, the man Christ Jesus; Who gave himself a ransom for all, to be testified in due time" (1 Timothy 2:5-6). The truly humble man will be receptive to what God has made known in His Word.

Through the infinite mercy of God the early church triumphed over these Satanic efforts to ally various dying cults and systems with Christianity. The Holy Ghost so clearly exposed them that in one council after another the church repudiated the vile theories that would have made man his own savior. But down through the centuries, from time to time there have been those who have taken up certain elements of these discarded schools of thought and sought to foist their theories on Christians as though they were new and wonderful truths. Romanism, with its doctrines of justification by works, purgatorial purification after death, and mediating saints and angels, has adopted much that the apostles refused, and palmed it off on credulous dupes as traditional Christianity. Imagine anyone praying to saints and angels or adoring their images when Colossians 2:18 says, "Let no man beguile you of your reward in a voluntary humility and worshipping of angels, intruding into those things which he hath not seen, vainly puffed up by his fleshly mind." How striking is the contrast between "voluntary humility" and "vainly puffed up"!

I remember trying to reason with a friend of my youth, a very gracious and kindly man who had been brought up from childhood in the Roman communion. Often I sought to show him from the Scriptures the simplicity of the gospel of Christ. When I asked why he prayed to the blessed virgin Mary instead of directly to our Lord Jesus, he answered with an air of the greatest humility, "Oh, I am too sinful, too utterly unworthy, to go directly to our blessed Lord. He is infinitely above me. He is so pure and holy and His majesty is so great that I would not dare to prostrate myself before Him. But I know that no one has as much influence with a son as his mother, and I know too that a pure woman's tender heart feels for sinners in their sorrows and failures. Therefore I go to the blessed virgin Mary and pour out my heart to her as I would to my own mother; I plead with her to speak for me to her holy, spotless Son. I feel sure that she will influence Him as no one else could."

This reasoning seems to reflect "lowliness of mind" and humility of spirit (Philippians 2:3), but it is really based on the most subtle kind of pride, for it involves the thought of being wiser than the revealed Word of God. There we read of only one mediator; there we learn that "the Father sent the Son to be the Saviour of the world" (1 John 4:14), that He bore "our sins in his own body on the tree" (1 Peter 2:24), and that His tender heart was filled with compassion for sinners here on earth. None was too vile or degraded to be invited to come to Him. The worst His enemies could say of Him was, "This man receiveth sinners, and eateth with them" (Luke 15:2).

Up yonder in glory He is the same Jesus that He was down here on earth. We may rest assured that "we have not an high priest which cannot be touched with the feeling of our infirmities, but was in all points tempted like as we are, yet without sin," and He is "able to succour them that are tempted." In His name we are bidden to "come boldly to the throne of grace, that we may obtain mercy, and find grace to help in time of need" (Hebrews 2:18; 4:15-16).

Since we are assured of Christ's deep interest in all that concerns us, why should we turn aside to angels or saints, however devoted, or even to His blessed mother herself when we can go directly to Him? He interceded for the transgressors on the cross and now at God's right hand He "ever liveth to make intercession" for those who trust in Him (Hebrews 7:25).

And so it is not an evidence of humility to say, "I am too unworthy to go to Christ." Only unbelief would lead one to make such a statement. He stands with arms outstretched, pleading with all who are in trouble or distress, "Come unto me, all ye that labour and are heavy laden, and I will give you rest" (Matthew 11:28). What base ingratitude to turn from Him to any other! Christ shows His wounded hands and says, "Peace be unto you" (Luke 24:36). What amazing folly to think it necessary to have anyone speak for me to Him! Only pride and unbelief would put Him at a distance and bring angels in between.

This "voluntary humility and worshipping of angels" is in itself a complete denial of the new creation, for it fails to recognize the wondrous truth that all believers are one body with their exalted Head. And so the apostle warned the Colossians about men "not holding the Head, from which all the body by joints and bands having nourishment ministered, and knit together, increaseth with the increase of God" (2:19). "Holding the Head" is recognizing our link with Him, both in life and by the Spirit. The exalted One at God's right hand is the source of blessing for all His people on earth. Just as the holy oil poured on Aaron's head went down to the skirts of his garment (Psalm 133:2), so now from the Head in Heaven blessing comes down in the Spirit's power to every member of His body on earth.

The body of Christ is not merely a society or an organization. It is far more wonderful. It is a divine organism. Just as all the members of a human body form the complete man, all believers in Christ, through the Spirit's baptism, form the one new man. (See 1 Corinthians 12:12-13 and Ephesians 2:15.)

If we are out of touch with the Head through failure to comprehend the intimacy of our relationship to Him, or if we put anything or any creature between ourselves and Him, we are not "holding the Head." Satan knows, as someone has well phrased it, that if he could get the thickness of a sheet of paper between the Head and the body, all life would be destroyed. The life of course can never be destroyed, but it is possible to utterly misunderstand our relationship to the Head and to fail to avail ourselves of the supplies of grace that might be ours if we walked in fellowship with Him; in such a sad condition we would be out of communion with Him and therefore not consciously guided by Him.

From the Head all the body is nourished through the ministry of "joints and bands" placed in the body by the Holy Spirit. Being thus "knit together," the body grows or increases (Colossians 2:19). This truth is most blessedly expanded and elaborated on in Ephesians 4:11-16. There we see how the risen Lord gave various gifts to His church "for the perfecting of the saints, for the work of the ministry, for the edifying of the body of Christ" (4:12). Note especially verses 15 and 16, where we are told that He would have us "grow up into him in all things, which is the head, even Christ: From whom the whole body fitly joined together and compacted by that which every joint supplieth, according to the effectual working in the measure of every part, maketh increase of the body unto the edifying of itself in love."

What a marvelous picture this is and how strikingly does one passage complement the other! Paul's words in Colossians and Ephesians put responsibility on each one of us as "members of Christ" and "members one of another" (1 Corinthians 6:15; Romans 12:5). There are no useless members in the body of Christ. In the human body every joint, every ligament, every hidden part, has some service to perform for the good of the whole. Even though physicians and surgeons may not yet fully understand the purpose of every gland and organ, and may speak of certain useless parts or of discarded vestiges of earlier forms, we may be sure that God in His infinite wisdom has a use for every part of the body. Likewise in the mystical body of Christ, no believer is useless or without a special gift. Therefore let no member of the body think of himself as having no part in building up the whole.

One term used in 1 Corinthians 12:28 is most suggestive; it is the little word "helps." Notice how it is sandwiched in between "gifts of healings" and "governments." We may not all have spectacular gifts, but we can all be helpers. For example the apostle spoke of "helping together by prayer" in 2 Corinthians 1:11. Prayer is a service the feeblest saint can perform for the benefit of the whole body.

If a member of the body of Christ is spiritually healthy, he will function properly for the edification of all. But just as a diseased part becomes a menace to the entire physical body, a Christian who is out of fellowship with God or in a low or carnal state, is a hindrance where he should be a helper. May each one of us be concerned about our responsibility to the body. May we be so focused on our blessed, glorified Head, so careful to see that there is nothing interfering with our communion with Him, that He may be able to use us to provide nourishment and blessing to His people. Then we all can be more "knit together" because of one another's faith and thus the body will grow.

Let me give some advice to my younger brothers in Christ who seek to preach the gospel or to labor for the edification of believers. Bear in mind that if you are true ministers of Jesus Christ, you will preach the Word and direct the attention of your hearers to the truth of God. Do not, I beg you, indulge in speculation about things not revealed. You are not sent forth to acquaint men with unsubstantiated theories or to fill their minds with philosophical systems. God has entrusted you with His own holy Word and He holds you responsible to declare it in all its clearness and simplicity. One "Thus saith the Lord" is worth a ton of human thoughts and ideas.

Unreliable theological treatises and philosophical discussions never saved one poor sinner or comforted a discouraged saint. It is the truth of God, declared in the power of the Holy Spirit, that alone can accomplish this. To teach anything else is to waste precious time and to dishonor the Lord who sent you out to proclaim His truth. The divinely given message, ministered in the power of the Holy Ghost sent down from Heaven, will awaken the careless, revive those who are "dead in trespasses and sins" (Ephesians 2:1), give peace to the anxious, comfort the distressed, and sanctify believers.

To substitute the empty dreams of carnal or unregenerate men for the truth of God is the utmost folly. Even in the Old Testament we read, "The prophet that hath a dream, let him tell a dream; and he that hath my word, let him speak my word faithfully. What is the chaff to the wheat? saith the Lord" (Jeremiah 23:28).

To add to His Word is to pervert it. Neither tradition, nor the voice of the church, nor imagined superior intellectual illumination can complete that which is already perfect: the revelation of the mind of God in His holy Word. The Bible and the Bible alone is the foundation of our faith.

Carnal Asceticism (Colossians 2:20-23)

The term *the flesh* is used in two very different senses in the Bible. It is a serious mistake to fail to distinguish between the two. Sometimes the term refers solely to our bodies—as in 2 Corinthians 4:11, "our mortal flesh"—but in the doctrinal parts of the New Testament the term generally refers to the nature that fallen man has inherited from his first father.

"God created man," we are told, "in his own image.... Male and female created he them...and called their name Adam, in the day when they were created" (Genesis 1:27; 5:2). Physically perfect, they were morally innocent and spiritually like God, who is a Spirit and the "Father of spirits" (Hebrews 12:9). But in Genesis 5:3 we read, "Adam...begat a son in his own likeness, after his image." Adam's children were born after sin had defiled his nature and poisoned the springs of life; and all his descendants now bear this fallen image.

As a result mankind needs regeneration and so our Lord said to Nicodemus, "That which is born of the flesh is flesh; and that which is born of the Spirit is spirit" (John 3:6). Jesus was not merely saying that that which is born of the physical body is a physical body; He was saying that the personality which comes into the world through natural procreation and birth has the fallen nature which Adam acquired when he fell. This fallen nature is distinctively referred to as the flesh, the body of the flesh, sin in the flesh, the sin that dwells in us, and as the carnal mind that is "not subject to the law of God, neither indeed can be" (Romans 8:7). *The flesh* in this sense is the nature of the old man, the unregenerate natural man. Ephesians 2:3 tells us that "we all...were by nature the children of wrath, even as others."

When a person is converted, or regenerated, this carnal nature is not altered in the slightest degree; it is never improved or sanctified, either in whole or in part. In the cross of Christ, God has utterly condemned the old nature as too vile for improvement. The believer has received a new nature that is spiritual, the nature of the new man; and he is now responsible to walk in obedience to the Word of God, which appeals only to this new nature. Both the old and the new natures are in the believer and will be until the redemption of the body.

It is true that the flesh, or the old nature, acts through the members of the body, but the body itself is not evil. However, every natural instinct and physical appetite, no matter how perfectly right and proper they may be when used as God intended, can be perverted to serve selfish and dishonorable purposes. So we are called on to "mortify [put to death] the deeds of the body" (Romans 8:13) and not to yield our "members as instruments of unrighteousness unto sin" (6:13). We are to present our bodies to God so that all their ransomed powers can be used for His service under the controlling power of His Holy Spirit.

Since the Christian is called to a life of self-abnegation, the apostle Paul wrote, "I keep under my body, and bring it into subjection" (1 Corinthians 9:27). But he did not mean that he needlessly punished his physical flesh in order to purify his spirit. He meant that he did not permit unlawful or inordinate physical appetites to dominate him and lead him into excesses that would dishonor his ministry and his Lord. This subjection of the body will always be necessary as long as we are in this world where we face temptations. First Peter 4:1 tells us, "He that hath suffered in the flesh hath ceased from sin." The thought here is not that we obtain deliverance from the power of sin by ascetic practices such as flagellation, fasting, or ignoring physical comfort. Peter meant that we obtain deliverance by refusing to obey carnal impulses that war against the soul while their gratification provides physical pleasure. Note the contrast between our Lord's temptation and our own. We read that He "suffered being tempted" (Hebrews 2:18), but we cease from sin if we suffer in the flesh. In other words, temptation caused Him, the holy One, the keenest suffering. His holy nature shrank from the slightest contact with evil—even from Satanic suggestion. But the suggestion of evil may be seductively pleasing to us, fallen as we are, and we must resolutely refuse the thought of sensual pleasure in order to walk in purity before God.

Hebrews 4:15 tells us that the Lord "was in all points tempted like as we are, yet without sin." In other words, He was never tempted by an inward desire for sin. He could say, "The prince of this world cometh, and hath nothing in me" (John 14:30). With us it is far otherwise; when temptation comes from without, we are sadly conscious of the fact that we have a traitor within who would open the door of the fortress to the enemy if he were not carefully watched. When the enemy attacks, our hearts must be determined to cleave to the Lord and give no ground to the suggestions of the flesh or the promptings of the adversary.

Someone explained the conflict between the two natures this way: "It seems to me as though two dogs are fighting within me. One is a black dog and he is very savage and very bad. The other is a white dog and he is very gentle and very good, but the black dog fights with him all the time."

"And which dog wins?" someone else asked.

"Whichever one I say *sic him* to."

His laconic reply was well-put, for if the will is on the side of the evil, the flesh will triumph; if the will is subdued by grace and subject to the Holy Spirit, the new nature will have control.

Because they lack understanding of this important truth, many have supposed that they could perfect themselves in holiness by imposing penances and various kinds of suffering on their bodies. Such views came into the church early in its history. The Jewish essenes and the stoic philosophers had accustomed both Jews and Gentiles to the thought that the body in itself is evil and must be subdued if one were to advance in holiness. This asceticism was advocated by certain sects of gnostics, while others went to the opposite extreme and taught that since the spirit alone was important, the body could be used in any way without polluting the soul.

In Colossians 2:20-23 the apostle Paul warned against the folly of seeking holiness through asceticism. He connected ascetic practices with the philosophies alluded to in verse 8, which he designated "the rudiments of the world." Challenging the believer, who as a new man in Christ has died with Him to his old place and condition in the world, Paul asked, "Wherefore if ye be dead with Christ from the rudiments of the world, why, as though living in the world, are ye subject to ordinances...after the commandments and doctrines of men?" All these rules and regulations for the subduing of the body are based on the principles of the world. They take for granted that God is still trying to improve the flesh, and this we know is not His purpose.

Through John the Baptist, God said, "The ax is laid unto the *root* of the trees" (Matthew 3:10, italics added). But from the early days of Christianity to modern times, men have used the ax, or the pruning knife, on the *fruit* of the trees, as though the trees might be improved if the bad fruit were cut off. Men say, "Get people to reform, to sign pledges, to put themselves under rules and regulations, to starve the body, to inflict physical suffering on it, and surely its vile propensities will be annulled if not eliminated. Little by little people will become spiritual and godlike." Thousands have agreed with the one who said, "Every day, in every way, / I am getting better and better." But no amount of self-control, no physical suffering whatever can change the carnal mind, which Scripture emphatically calls *the flesh.*

Saint Jerome lived a lecherous life in his youth, but after he became a Christian he fled from all contact with the gross and vulgar world in which he had once sought to gratify every fleshly desire. He left Rome, wandered to Palestine, and lived in a cave near Bethlehem, where he sought to subdue his carnal nature by fasting almost to starvation. So he was greatly disappointed when, exhausted and weary, he fell asleep and dreamed he was still rioting among the dissolute companions of his godless days.

The flesh cannot be starved into subjection. It cannot be improved by subjecting it to ordinances, whether human or divine. But as we walk in the Spirit and fill our minds with thoughts of the risen Christ, we are delivered from the power of "fleshly lusts, which war against the soul" (1 Peter 2:11).

In the parenthetical portion of Colossians 2:20-23 the apostle gave examples of carnal ordinances: "Touch not; taste not; handle not" (2:21). He was not saying, "Do not touch, taste, or handle these ascetic regulations." That would be nonsense. He was giving examples of human rules, through obedience to which the ascetic hoped to attain a higher degree of spirituality. Often we hear verse 21 quoted as guidance for Christians, but the apostle's intention was exactly the opposite. He wanted all such regulations "to perish with the using" (2:22).

Subjection to human rules gives an appearance of wisdom. It is natural to suppose that neglecting or punishing the body would have a tendency to free one from carnal desires, but untold thousands of monks, hermits, and ascetics of all descriptions, have proved that such practices are useless in preventing indulgence of the flesh. When a man shuts himself up in a monastery in order to escape the world, he finds that he has brought the world in with him. If he were to dwell in a cave in the desert in order to subdue the flesh, he would only find that the more the body is weakened and neglected, the more powerful the flesh becomes.

Dr. A. T. Robertson translated the last part of Colossians 2:20 and all of 2:21 as follows: "Why, as though living in the world, do you dogmatize; such as, Touch not; taste not; handle not?" Such rules may be elevated to the importance of dogmas, but they will never enable one to achieve his goal.

A story is told of a man who was anxious to make himself fit to

enter the presence of God. Awakened to a sense of the emptiness of
a life of worldly pleasure, he fled from the city to the desert and
made his home in a cave in the rocks. There he practiced the greatest austerities and hoped through prayer and penance to reach the
place where he would be acceptable to God. Hearing of another
hermit who was reputed to be very holy and devout, the man took
his staff and made a long, wearisome journey across the desert in
order to interview him and learn from him how to find peace with
God. In answer to the man's agonized questions the aged hermit
said, "Take that staff, that dry rod which is in your hand, and plant
it in the desert soil. Water it daily, offering fervent prayers as you
do so, and when it bursts into leaf and bloom, you will know that
you have made your peace with God."

Rejoicing that at last he had what seemed like authoritative instruction in regard to this greatest of all ventures, the man hastened
back to his cave and planted his rod as he had been told to do. For
long weary days, weeks, and months, he faithfully watered the dry
stick and prayed for the hour when the token of his acceptance would
be given. He continued this routine until at last one day in utter
despair and brokenness of spirit, weakened by fasting and sick with
longing for the apparently unattainable, he exclaimed bitterly, "It is
all no use; I am no better today than I was when I first came to the
desert. The fact is, I am just like this dry stick myself. It needs life
before there can be leaves and fruit; and I need life, for I am dead in
my sins and cannot produce fruit for God."

And then it seemed as though a voice within said, "At last you
have learned the lesson that the old hermit meant to teach you. It is
because you are dead and have no strength or power in yourself that
you must turn to Christ alone and find life and peace in Him." And
leaving his desert cave, the man went back to the city to find the
Word of God and in its sacred pages learn the way of peace.

Let us remember that it is as impossible to obtain holiness by
ascetic practices as it is to buy salvation by physical suffering. We
are saved in the first place, not through anything we undergo, but
through that which our blessed Lord Jesus Christ underwent for us
on Calvary's cross. He who died for our justification now lives for

us at God's right hand, and He is the power that produces holiness in us. By the Holy Spirit He dwells within us and as we yield ourselves to God, He is enabled to live out His wondrous life in us. Does your heart sometimes cry:

Tell me what to do to be pure
In the sight of the all-seeing eyes;
Tell me, is there no thorough cure,
No escape from the sin I despise?

. . . .
Will my Saviour only pass by,
Only show me how faulty I've been?
Will he not attend to my cry?
Can I not at this moment be clean?
(Samuel Horatio Hodges)

Oh, believe me, dear anxious, seeking Christian, you will find holiness in the same Christ in whom you found salvation. As you cease from introspection and look up in faith to Him, you will be transformed into His own glorious image; you will become like Him as you gaze on His wonderful face. There is no other way by which the flesh can be subdued and your life can become one of triumph over the power of sin. Asceticism is but a vain will-o'-the-wisp that, while it promises you victory, will plunge you into the morass of disappointment and defeat. But preoccupation with the risen Christ is the sure way to overcome the lusts of the flesh and to become like Him who said, "For their sakes I sanctify myself, that they also might be sanctified through the truth" (John 17:19).

People said that Jesus was a glutton and a winebibber (Matthew 11:19) because He came not as an ascetic, but as a man among men, entering with them into every sinless experience of human life. He left us an example that we should follow (1 Peter 2:21). He came to sanctify every natural relationship, not to do violence to the affections and feelings that He Himself implanted in the hearts of mankind.

CHAPTER THREE
CHRIST, THE BELIEVER'S LIFE

Power for Holiness (Colossians 3:1-4)

After the somewhat lengthy digression in Colossians 2:13-23, the apostle turned his attention to applying the truth taught in 2:12. I think we can see the connection better if we read 2:12 and 3:1 without anything intervening: "Buried with him in baptism, wherein also ye are risen with him through the faith of the operation of God, who hath raised him from the dead....If ye then be risen with Christ, seek those things which are above, where Christ sitteth on the right hand of God." The digression in 2:13-23 was a warning against false systems that try to rob the believer of the great truth of unity with Christ in death and resurrection.

It is all-important that we realize that we do not stand before God on the ground of responsibility. The responsible man failed utterly to keep his obligations and thus there was nothing for him but condemnation. But our Lord Jesus Christ has borne that condemnation; in infinite grace He voluntarily took the place of the sinner and bore his punishment on the cross. Now in resurrection the believer is not only presented by Him as perfect before the throne of God; he is also found to be "in Christ" by virtue of being a partaker of His life. Once he was "in Adam," having been born of his race, but now he is "in Christ." The contrast clearly indicates that he has received a new life from Him and therefore he is not to think of himself in any sense as on probation. All legalism was ended on the cross of Christ.

> Jesus died and we died with Him,
> Buried in His grace we lay,
> One in Him in resurrection,
> Soon with Him in Heaven's bright day.
>
> Death and judgment are behind us,
> Grace and glory are before;
> All the billows rolled o'er Jesus,
> There exhausted all their power.

The death of Christ, in which faith has given the believer a part, has severed the link that bound him to the world and all its purposes and has freed him from all necessity to be subject to sin. When he realizes this fact, he is free to glorify God as he walks in newness of life. Since most theological systems fail to explain this great truth of the new man in Christ, few believers have a settled peace and few realize their union with Him who sits at God's right hand, not only as the Head of the church but also as the Head of every man who has found life through Him.

Centering our thoughts on Christ—Christ risen in the energy of the Holy Spirit—is the means of obtaining power for holiness. We are called on to "seek those things which are above, where Christ sitteth on the right hand of God." Our real life is there; our truest, best interests are all identified with Him. Heavenly-mindedness is the natural or I should say spiritual outcome of realizing our union with the risen Christ. As our hearts are absorbed with Him we will be concerned about representing Him well in this world where He is still rejected and His claims are still refused.

In the King James version Colossians 3:2 reads, "Set your affection on things above, not on things on the earth." A better translation would be "Set your mind on things above, not on things on the earth." As a watch is set according to the sun in order to mark the time correctly, we are to let our minds be set to the risen Christ so that His life may be seen in us. Since we are now one with the risen Christ, the time for minding earthly things is past (note the contrast between Colossians 3:2 and Philippians 3:19).

Fixing our minds on heavenly things will not make us impractical and visionary. Rather, we will live all the more consistently as we fulfill our varied responsibilities in the home, in business, in the state, and of course in the church. We will reveal the heavenly character just where we come closest into contact with the things of the earth.

During the forty days between resurrection and ascension, Christ was still here on the earth, but He was altogether heavenly (see 2 Corinthians 5:16). Likewise we are called into association with Him to reveal the heavenly character while we are still walking the desert sands. Men of the world will not understand us and we need not expect them to. Nevertheless they can and will recognize and appreciate true piety and Christian character even though they hate those who possess it, just as Cain hated Abel "because his own works were evil, and his brother's righteous" (1 John 3:12). But it should be true of us, as it was of our blessed Lord, that this hatred is undeserved. Jesus said that in fulfillment of prophecy, "They hated me without a cause" (John 15:25).

As Colossians 3:3 indicates, we have died to all that we once were as children of Adam, and now as Christians we do not have independent life, but Christ Himself is our life. And while it is true we have this eternal life abiding in us, He who is the source and sustainer of it is hidden yonder in the heavens "in God," and so our life is safe in His keeping.

We can appreciate the remark of a simple brother who had been greatly concerned after his conversion that by some sinful act or lack of faith he might in some way forfeit his salvation and lose the new life that had in grace been given to him. As he listened to an address based on Colossians 3:3, his anxiety disappeared and he exclaimed with rapture, "Glory to God! Whoever heard of a man drowning with his head that high above water!" Admittedly his words were crude; nevertheless they expressed a great truth. Our Head is in Heaven and our life is in Him, who is hidden in God; therefore we are eternally one with Him and nothing can ever separate the Christian from the risen Christ.

Believers in the Lord Jesus are like other men outwardly. They are still in dying bodies, they are often distressed by the carnal nature within, and they are often in conflict with Satan and the world without. Yet each believer is called to walk through this world in the power of resurrection life, reflecting his union with his glorified Head. He is called to be a man of God, even in the midst of the humblest circumstances.

> There is no glory halo
> Round his devoted head,
> No luster marks the sacred path
> In which his footsteps tread.

> But holiness is graven
> Upon his thoughtful brow,
> And all his steps are ordered
> In the light of Heaven e'en now.

> He often is peculiar,
> And oft misunderstood,
> And yet his power is felt by all—
> The evil and the good.

> For he doth live in touch with Heaven
> A life of faith and prayer;
> His hope, his purpose, and his all,
> His life is centered there.

Such a person is indeed a consistent member of the body of Christ, for he displays the character of the new man whose Head is in Heaven. And although the Christian may, like his Lord, be despised and rejected by men, he is called to run with patience the race set before him, knowing that the day is nearing when he too will receive satisfaction (see Isaiah 53:3,11; Hebrews 12:1). Christ will find His satisfaction in us and we will find ours in Him.

> He and I in that bright glory
> One deep joy shall share:

Mine, to be forever with Him,
His, that I am there!
(Gerhard Tersteegen)

When the day of the Lord dawns after earth's long, dark night—
or to put it another way, after man's garish day is ended—those
who have been content to be strangers and pilgrims here during
Christ's rejection will shine forth with Him as He comes to reign as
King of kings and Lord of lords. And so Paul wrote to the Colossian
saints, "When Christ, who is our life, shall appear, then shall ye
also appear with him in glory" (3:4). When He with whom we have
died and in whom we are risen returns from Heaven and is displayed before His earthly people who have been waiting for Him,
and before His foes as well, we too will be displayed with Him in
glory.

His coming is presented to us in two aspects in the New Testament and the aspect that perhaps most appeals to every real lover of
Christ is what we commonly call the rapture. Our hearts long for
the hour when "the Lord himself shall descend from heaven with a
shout, with the voice of the archangel, and with the trump of God:
and the dead in Christ shall rise first: Then we which are alive and
remain shall be caught up together with them in the clouds, to meet
the Lord in the air" (1 Thessalonians 4:16-17).

We think of the rapture as the end of the race and as the time
when He will "change our vile body, that it may be fashioned like
unto his glorious body" (Philippians 3:21). At the time of the rapture "this corruptible [will] put on incorruption, and this mortal [will]
put on immortality" (1 Corinthians 15:53) and we will be fully "conformed to the image of [God's] Son" (Romans 8:29). The promise
made by our Lord before He went away will be fulfilled: "I go to
prepare a place for you. And if I go and prepare a place for you, I
will come again, and receive you unto myself; that where I am,
there ye may be also" (John 14:2-3). The rapture will be the occasion of our reception into the Father's house.

All of this is calculated to stir the souls of His waiting ones to
their deepest depths, but blessed as it is, the rapture is but an introduction to the glories yet to be revealed in the everlasting kingdom

of our Lord and Savior Jesus Christ. He is coming back to the earth that rejected Him, and all His saints are coming with Him—but not of course to resume human life under the same conditions. It is in resurrection bodies that they will appear with Him before the astonished eyes of those who still reject Him and to the delight of those who are waiting for Him as the delivering King. In that day Revelation 1:7 will be fulfilled: "Behold, he cometh with clouds; and every eye shall see him, and they also which pierced him: and all kindreds of the earth shall wail because of him."

In Colossians 3:4 Paul referred to this time when we will "appear with him in glory" and he referred to it again in 2 Thessalonians 1:5-11, where he offered comfort to the suffering saints. The apostle assured them that God will recompense tribulation to their persecutors and that rest will be the portion of the redeemed

> when the Lord Jesus shall be revealed from heaven with his mighty angels, In flaming fire taking vengeance on them that know not God, and that obey not the gospel of our Lord Jesus Christ: Who shall be punished with everlasting destruction from the presence of the Lord, and from the glory of his power; When he shall come to be glorified in his saints, and to be admired in all them that believe (because our testimony among you was believed) in that day (2 Thessalonians 1:7-10).

The parenthetical words "because our testimony among you was believed" explain why any from among earth's inhabitants will be associated with Christ in the glory of that day.

> Lamb of God, Thou soon in glory
> Wilt to this sad earth return;
> All Thy foes shall quake before Thee,
> All that now despise Thee, mourn.

> Then shall we, at Thine appearing,
> With Thee in Thy kingdom reign;
> Thine the praise and Thine the glory,
> Lamb of God for sinners slain!

This is the consummation to which the Christian dispensation is leading: the kingdoms of this world will become the kingdoms of our God and of His Christ (Revelation 11:15) and His one-time pilgrim people will reign with Him in righteousness throughout Messiah's glorious years.

What a gospel we have! Surely it was never conceived in the mind of man. It could not have been, for it makes nothing of man but everything of Christ. May we dwell on it more and more as the days grow darker and the end draws near. May we "look not at the things which are seen, but at the things which are not seen" (2 Corinthians 4:18) as we live in daily expectation of Christ's return to take us to be with Himself and make us fully like Himself forevermore.

> For God has fixed the happy day,
> When the last tear shall dim our eyes,
> When He will wipe these tears away,
> And fill our hearts with glad surprise.
> To hear His voice, and see His face,
> And know the fulness of His grace.

The blessed consummation of all our hopes is clearly presented in the Word of God so that we may be heartened and lifted above discouragement and the depressing power of present sorrows, whether in the world or the church. Thus cheered by the glory shining from the gates of the heavenly city, we may run the race with patience, ever "looking unto Jesus" (Hebrews 12:1-2).

The apostle completed the doctrinal teaching of the Epistle in Colossians 3:4 and turned to practical considerations in 3:5.

The Old Ways (Colossians 3:5-11)

While the first part of Colossians is doctrinal (1:1–3:4), the second part (3:5–4:18) is practical, emphasizing the importance of walking in the power of the truth of the new man and our relationship to Christ as Head. In the second part, the first passage—

Colossians 3:5-17—deals with practical holiness in relation to our-selves (3:5-11) and in relation to others (3:12-17). Verses 5-11 challenge the individual to "put off" the old ways; then verses 12 to 17 present the claims of Christian fellowship. The sequence is significant, for we must be right in our own inner lives if we want to be right in our relationships with our brothers in Christ. Proverbs 4:23 says, "Keep thy heart with all diligence; for out of it are the issues of life." What I am when I am alone in the presence of God, is what I really am. What I am when I am with other people, should be the same; otherwise my public life is largely a sham. The measurements of the fine linen in the tabernacle are sugges-tive of this line of reasoning. The tabernacle, as we know, was pri-marily a wonderful type of our Lord Jesus Christ. It was God's dwelling place and we read, "The Word was made flesh, and dwelt [tabernacled] among us, (and we beheld his glory, the glory as of the only begotten of the Father,) full of grace and truth" (John 1:14).

Surrounding the court of the tabernacle were curtains of fine twined linen suspended from pillars. Fine linen, we learn from Rev-elation 19:8, represents "the righteous acts of the saints" (literal rendering). Therefore the linen surrounding the court spoke of the perfect ways of our Lord Jesus Christ on earth, which were seen by men. These hangings were visible to all, but inside the tabernacle, covering the upright boards, which were made of acacia wood and overlaid with gold, were ten more curtains of fine twined linen and these were not visible to men on the outside. The inside curtains, which were seen only by God (and His ministering priests in meas-ure), spoke of Christ's perfect righteousness as seen by God the Father.

Christ's righteousness on earth led men to exclaim, "He hath done all things well" (Mark 7:37), and caused even Pilate to declare, "I find no fault in him" (John 19:4). The perfection that the Father saw caused Him to open the heavens and proclaim, "This is my beloved Son, in whom I am well pleased" (Matthew 3:17).

Now how many cubits of fine twined linen formed the wall sur-rounding the court of the tabernacle? The court was 100 cubits long and 50 cubits wide (300 cubits altogether), so if we subtract 20 cu-bits for the varicolored gate of the tabernacle, the difference is 280 cubits: 100 on each side, 50 in the rear, and 30 in front. And how many cubits of fine twined linen covered the upright boards of the tabernacle itself? These ten inside curtains were each 28 cubits long; these were joined together, making a total of 280 cubits. So there were 280 cubits of fine twined linen where all could see it, and 280 cubits where only God could see it in its completeness. What a lesson is suggested by these facts! Our blessed Lord was just the same before God as He was before men. When His enemies came asking, "Who art thou?" He answered, "Even the same that I said unto you" (John 8:25). With Him profession and life were in perfect agreement, and this is the standard that God now sets for the believer.

But the width of the inside curtains was different from the width of the hangings surrounding the court and this fact is also suggestive. The inside curtains were four cubits wide; the number four is symbolic of weakness and therefore the width of the curtains speaks of Christ's perfect subjection to the will of the Father. The hangings outside were five cubits wide; the number five is symbolic of responsibility and therefore the width of the hangings speaks of our Lord's taking the place of responsibility here on earth, as He met every claim of God that man had flouted.

Recognizing our union with Christ, we are called on to show forth His life. First we must put to death all of our old ways. We have identified with Christ in His death; in the cross we were circumcised with the circumcision of Christ (Colossians 2:11); therefore we are to mortify our members which are upon the earth (3:5). The believer is never told to crucify himself; he is told to mortify the members of his body. We have been "crucified with Christ" and "they that are Christ's have crucified the flesh with the affections and lusts" (Galatians 2:20; 5:24). All the old ways passed under judgment in the cross, but to make this truth practical the flesh must be kept, by faith, in the place of death and its evil promptings must be refused in self-judgment.

The apostle insisted on the importance of dealing unsparingly with the sins that were so common in the heathen world out of which the Colossians had been saved. Unfortunately these sins are almost as common in today's world in spite of increased light and civilization. The believer, recognizing his link with Christ, is to abhor all uncleanness. He is to remember that "the body is…for the Lord; and the Lord for the body" (1 Corinthians 6:13). The believer is to mortify every tendency to commit the sins mentioned in Colossians 3:5: "Fornication, uncleanness, inordinate affection, evil concupiscence [unlawful lusts], and covetousness, which is idolatry [for in reality it is the worship of self]." All these are to be judged in the light of the cross of Christ, no matter what the cost. No excuse is to be offered for such sins and no palliation of their wickedness is to be attempted on the basis of the innate tendencies of human nature. These sins are abhorrent to God and abhorrent to the new nature in every believer. "For which things' sake," Colossians 3:6 tells us, "the wrath of God cometh on the children of disobedience." As we read this verse we remember that God destroyed the antediluvian world because of corruption and violence, and rained fire from heaven on the cities of the plain because of unbridled lust and passion.

The Colossians had once lived unblushingly in these sins that are so characteristic of men away from God. But that was before they knew Christ. Now, having risen with Him and having seen these things in their true light, the Colossians needed to reject them as dishonoring to God and contrary to Christ. Other sins may have seemed to them to be far less vile and abominable than those mentioned in Colossians 3:5, but these too needed to be mortified. They were the habits of the old man, his old clothes that were not fit to adorn the new man. And so Paul wrote, "Also put off all these; anger, wrath, malice, blasphemy, filthy communication out of your mouth. Lie not one to another, seeing that ye have put off the old man with his deeds" (3:8-9).

The old man is more than the old nature. It is the man I used to be before I knew Christ as Savior and Lord. In other words, the old man is all that I once was as an unsaved person. I am through with that man; he has disappeared in the cross of Christ. But if I make this profession of faith, let me be sure that I do not walk in the old man's ways. Sometimes those who make the loudest professions of the truth of the new creation are the poorest performers of the truth; they give the lie to what they say by what they do. We could borrow the words of Ralph Waldo Emerson and say to them, "What you *are*...thunders so that I cannot hear what you say." I am afraid that many a Christian has lost his testimony because of carelessness in his walk.

Paul said to "put off...anger, wrath, malice." Anger, as we know from Ephesians 4:26, may be righteous, but generally it is the raging of the flesh. Even where anger is warranted (as in Mark 3:5 where we read that our blessed Lord looked at His opponents with anger because of the hardness of their hearts), it must not be nursed or it will degenerate into wrath. Wrath, a settled condition of ill-feeling toward an offender, is generally coupled with a desire for revenge and so malice springs from it. We have three generations of sin here: anger cherished begets wrath, and wrath if not judged begets malice. No matter how grievously I have been wronged, I am not to yield to the devil and malign or seek to harm the one against whom I may have been righteously indignant in the beginning. "Let not the sun go down upon your wrath: Neither give place to the devil" (Ephesians 4:26-27).

We are also to "put off...blasphemy." This dreadful sin may be directed either godward or manward. Men blaspheme against God by imputing evil to Him, or by seeking to misrepresent Him, or by perverting the truth about the Father, the Son, or the Spirit. But speaking injuriously of one another, reviling rulers or governors, circulating wicked and untruthful reports about one's brothers, and seeking to harm God's servants by such evil reports—all these are also included under the general term *blasphemy*. Sharp-tongued religious controversialists have often failed here, even at the very moment that they were endeavoring to meet the blasphemy of their opponents in regard to divine things.

When one hyper-Calvinist described John Wesley as a child of the devil because of his Arminianism, the Calvinist himself had fallen into the sin of blasphemy. No wonder his son, William Hone, turned from Christianity and was an infidel for years until he was reached by divine grace. It is incongruous for bitter accusations to come from the lips of those who have been saved through mercy alone and daily need to confess their own sins and ask for divine forgiveness. "The wrath of man worketh not the righteousness of

God" (James 1:20). The holy One is not honored by our hard
speeches against His saints — or even against men of the world.
Paul finished Colossians 3:8 by saying that we should "put
off...filthy communication." If we did not know the corruption of
our own hearts, we might think that it was unnecessary for the apostle
to warn redeemed saints against the vice of using unclean language
or relating salacious stories. Christians should shun questionable
stories and the repetition of details (true or false) that only tend to
feed the old nature.

Once I heard someone begin a story with the remark, "As there
are no ladies here, I want to tell you something I heard the other
day." Another gentleman in the group checked him with a wise answer: "Brother, though there are no ladies present, the Holy Ghost
is here. Is your story fit for Him?" The first man blushed in confu-
sion and accepted the rebuke. We did not hear the story.

Colossians 3:9 adds, "Lie not one to another, seeing that ye have
put off the old man with his deeds." If there were any truth in the
unscriptural theory held by some that the old nature is eradicated
when a believer is sanctified, there would be no need for this injunction.

Lying is one of the first evidences of the carnal nature. "The
wicked...go astray as soon as they be born, speaking lies" (Psalm
58:3) and untruthfulness is one of the hardest habits for anyone to
overcome. It is so natural for these vain hearts of ours to try to make
things appear better than they really are, to cover up our own failures and accentuate the sins of others. But these are just different
forms of lying and we are called on to judge all guile—every kind
of untruthfulness—in the light of the cross of Christ. There the old
man was crucified in the person of our Substitute, and now his deeds
are to be renounced and his habits put off as discarded garments,
which are in no sense fit for the new man.

The new man, we gather from Colossians 3:10-11, is the man
in Christ, just as the old man was the man in Adam. The new
man has a new, divinely-imparted nature, and it is to this new
nature that God, by the Spirit, appeals; only the new nature is
capable of receiving divine instruction. As such instruction is

imparted and the truths thus received control the life, the believer increasingly displays the image of Him who is the Head of the new creation, who Himself is "the image of the invisible God" (Colossians 1:15).

Man was created in the image and likeness of God in the beginning, but that image became terribly marred through sin. In the new man this image again becomes visible and the characteristics of Christ are seen in His people. This is true regardless of who or what they were before they received the new life—whether they were cultured Greeks or religious Jews; whether they were within the circle of the Abrahamic covenant, marked off from the rest of humanity by the ordinance of circumcision, or outside the circle and strangers to the covenants of promise; whether they were barbarian or Scythian (that is, of the wild tribes outside the boundaries of civilization); whether they were slaves or free citizens. All alike were sinners; all alike were included in the old man.

Now those who through grace have believed the gospel are members of the new creation. No matter what they were before, God sees them as justified from all things. They possess a new and divine life and they belong to that new company where Christ is everything and in everyone. The Christian recognizes that there still are racial and class distinctions in this world, but he knows that more important than his earthly status is his new place in Christ.

New responsibilities flow from being linked up with the new Head. Because he is a new-creation man, the Christian is called on to adopt new ways and to develop new habits—to put on new clothes suited to his new relationship.

However, the new creation is not simply an individual matter. It is not merely that I, as a believer, am a new creature in Christ Jesus. In the King James version, 2 Corinthians 5:17 reads, "If any man be in Christ, he is a new creature...," but a better rendering would be "If any man be in Christ, it is new creation: old things are passed away; behold, all things are become new." Not yet do we see all the evidence of the new creation, but "we see Jesus,...crowned with glory and honour," seated above the changing scenes of time (Hebrews 2:9).

Joyful now the new creation
Rests in undisturbed repose;
Blest in Jesus' full salvation
Sorrow now nor thraldom knows.

Until He returns, we who are members of the new creation are called on to show by our new ways the holiness, the grace, the righteousness, the love, and the compassion of Christ. He is the origin and the Head of the new creation, where all things are of God. We find another reference to the new creation in Galatians 6:15-16: "In Christ Jesus neither circumcision availeth any thing, nor uncircumcision, but a new creature [or a new creation]. And as many as walk according to this rule [the controlling principle of this new creation], peace be on them, and mercy, and upon the Israel of God." This is the very opposite of legality. Walking according to the controlling principle of the new creation is the spontaneous expression of the life of the Head in the members here on earth.

Garments of Glory (Colossians 3:12-17)

This passage talks about our new clothes, the garments of the new man—the things we are to put on in place of the old habits we have discarded. Both Scripture and ordinary Anglo-Saxon language sometimes use the same words in reference to both clothing and behavior. We speak of habits of various descriptions, meaning clothing worn on particular occasions—a riding habit, a walking habit—and we speak of our behavior as our habit. When Solomon says, "Let thy garments be always white" (Ecclesiastes 9:8), we of course understand him to mean, "Let your habits or behavior be pure and righteous." The wicked are depicted as "clothed with filthy garments" and self-righteousness is described as "filthy rags" (Zechariah 3:3; Isaiah 64:6). But the characteristics of the newborn man are garments of glory and beauty.

It is a common saying that you can judge a man by his clothes, but this is not always true. Many a princely character has, because of poverty, been obliged to dress in worn-out and unbecoming garments, while rascals of the deepest dye have arrayed themselves like princes of royal blood. Nor is the saying always true in regard to the behavior of children of God and the unsaved. Wolves sometimes come in sheep's clothing, ministers of Satan can appear to be ministers of righteousness, and real believers may have garments that are badly stained and torn by failure and sin. But ordinarily men are judged according to their appearance, and Christians are expected to be adorned with good works. Thus they give credibility to the profession they make of justification before God by faith in Jesus Christ. Faith and works are the two sides of truth emphasized by the apostle Paul in his Epistle to the Romans and by James the Lord's brother in his intensely practical letter.

What kind of habits or behavior should characterize the man in Christ? With what beautiful garments should he be arrayed? First of all we read, "Put on therefore, as the elect of God, holy and beloved, bowels of mercies" (Colossians 3:12). "The elect of God" are those whom He has foreknown from all eternity and who are shown in time to be believers in His Son. God sees them as "holy and beloved." They have been set apart in Christ—sanctified by the blood of the everlasting covenant. They are dear to God because they are His own children; they are partakers of the divine nature. How unseemly it would be if these "holy and beloved" ones were ever stern and unfeeling toward others when they themselves are recipients of grace!

The Old Testament writers used the term *bowels* the way we use the word *heart* in reference to the deepest feelings of humanity. Instead of "bowels of mercies," we might read "emotions of pity." While this may not be exactly a translation, it at least expresses in English the thought of the original. We are called on to have hearts that are readily stirred to feel compassion. Like God Himself, we are to delight in mercy. We may well question whether an unmerciful person has really been born of God.

Harshness in dealing with failing brethren is not the spirit of Christ. Yearning love should characterize our dealings with one another. Such love will lead us to go to great lengths to be merciful if it is possible to do so without opposing God's righteous claims. First Peter 3:8 says, "Be pitiful," and how much we need to take such an exhortation to heart! The cruelest things have been done in the name of Him who is the incarnation of infinite mercy. How often Christ's attitude toward sin and sinners has been misrepresented by those who profess to be His followers! Christ's attitude was one of "kindness," and this is the next word in Colossians 3:12. It is quite impossible to maintain fellowship with God and not show the kindness of God to others. There may indeed be a rigid, legalistic type of piety that leads one to imagine that he has been appointed by God to demonstrate His justice, but this kind of piety is far from the godliness advocated in the New Testament. Macaulay said of some of the sterner Puritans, "As one reads their writings he wonders if they had ever read a little volume called the New Testament." The lovingkindness of the Lord will be revealed in our kindness to one another.

The garments of pity and kindness are, we might say, inner vestments. The next one is a cap for the head, "humbleness of mind." Pride is of all things the most hateful to God. Psalm 138:6 tells us, "The proud he knoweth afar off," and Proverbs 16:18 says, "Pride goeth before destruction, and an haughty spirit before a fall."

The realization of one's own weakness and natural tendency to err will lead to low thoughts of self and make it easy to don the vesture of "meekness." This grace is composed of rarer material than is often supposed. Our Lord was adorned with it; He could say, "I am meek and lowly in heart." How beautiful He appeared thus arrayed. Moses had a garment of this excellent texture, lawgiver though he was, for we read, "The man Moses was very meek, above all the men which were upon the face of the earth" (Numbers 12:3). So delicate is this fabric that it can easily wear away in the stress and strain of the trials of life; therefore one needs to be constantly seeking for meekness, which can only be found in communion with God. In Zephaniah 2:3 the prophet told the "meek of the earth" to "seek meekness." Matthew 11:29 suggests the necessity of coming under Christ's control if we want to be adorned with meekness: "Take my yoke upon you, and learn of me; for I am meek and lowly in heart."

The world will never understand the value of the lowly spirit. Our own lionhearted Theodore Roosevelt once said, "I hate a meek man." He probably did not realize that the boldest man, the most utterly unafraid man ever seen on earth, was our Lord Jesus Christ, who was in the fullest sense a meek man. Meekness, which is not inconsistent with bravery, enables one to suffer and be strong when the world would "turn aside the way of the meek" (Amos 2:7).

Closely associated with meekness is the grace of "longsuffering," which is the readiness to endure the grief of suffering wrongfully. When we are falsely accused, it is natural for us to resent such treatment or to feel that we must defend ourselves. But when false witnesses rose up against our blessed Lord, He answered not a word. And when the adversary taunted King Hezekiah and his officers, charged them falsely, and threatened severe treatment, the king's command to his people was, "Answer him not" (2 Kings 18:36).

God can be depended on to vindicate His own if they do not attempt to vindicate themselves. As they learn to commit their reputation—as well as everything else that they once considered valuable—to Christ, they can patiently endure mistreatment without resentment and pray for those who despitefully use them and persecute them (Matthew 5:44). In longsuffering, believers become consistent followers of the Man of Sorrows who could say, "They laid to my charge things that I knew not" (Psalm 35:11).

Colossians 3:13 reads, "Forbearing one another, and forgiving one another, if any man have a quarrel against any: even as Christ forgave you, so also do ye." Paul expressed the same thought in Ephesians 4:32: "Be ye kind one to another, tenderhearted, forgiving one another, even as God for Christ's sake [or, in Christ] hath forgiven you."

When teaching His disciples to pray, our Lord told them to say, "Forgive us our debts, as we forgive our debtors," and He added, "If ye forgive not men their trespasses, neither will your Father forgive your trespasses" (Matthew 6:12,15). The forgiveness the disciples were to seek was not the forgiveness of a sinner, but the forgiveness of a failing saint, one who could address God as "our Father." In effect our Lord was saying to the disciples: "You are failing from day to day; you constantly need your Father's restorative forgiveness. Yet you cherish feelings of malice and enmity and an unforgiving spirit toward your brothers who offend you. If you do not forgive them, you cannot expect your Father's forgiveness when you come to Him confessing your failures. As long as you cherish this spirit of malice, you cannot really pray in faith."

On the other hand, Colossians 3:13 and Ephesians 4:32 speak of the forgiveness of a sinner. Paul was saying, "Think how freely you have been forgiven. In the light of how much God has cast behind His back (Isaiah 38:17), how can you have hard feelings or maintain an unforgiving spirit toward those who have sinned against you? If God had dealt with you according to your offenses, how fearful would your judgment be! Yet He in Christ has graciously forgiven them all. He has put away every sin and made you fit for His holy presence. Your responsibility now is to forgive as you have been forgiven."

In his novel *The Man from Glengarry* Ralph Connor told the striking story of the conversion of Macdonald Dubh. I understand that the incident is founded on actual fact and is not merely fiction. Macdonald—a powerful, burly highlander living in Glengarry County, Ontario—had for years suffered untold anguish because of an injury inflicted on him by a French Canadian. Macdonald had nursed the desire to take fearful vengeance on his foe until the desire became an obsession. Neither God nor eternity had any place in Macdonald's life. Trying to persuade him to forgive his enemy, the minister's wife would ask him to repeat the Lord's prayer, but he always balked at the words, "Forgive us our trespasses as we forgive those that trespass against us."

But there was a great revival in Glengarry County. As God worked in power, real Christians were aroused and christless men and women were saved. The story of the cross, told by the venerable highland minister in the Gaelic tongue, broke Macdonald's heart and bowed him in penitence at the Savior's feet. The next time the minister's wife went to visit him and tried to stress the necessity of forgiveness, he sobbed out, "Oh, it's a little thing, it's a little thing, for I have been forgiven so much!" He could now say the Lord's prayer without balking.

Christ's forgiveness grips the heart and enables one to bear in patience the ill-doing and evil-speaking of others and preserves one from bitterness of spirit or any desire for vengeance. How can anyone who has been forgiven for so much ever harbor an unforgiving spirit?

Turning to Colossians 3:14, we read, "Above all these things put on charity, which is the bond of perfectness." Here we have the belt that holds all our new garments in place. The verse might be rendered, "Over all these things put on love, which is the girdle of perfection." Just as the oriental binds his flowing robes about him with a sash, so the new man binds his new habits with the controlling power of love. Whatever is contrary to love is contrary to Christ. No amount of sophistry can make something pleasing to God if it is opposed to the divine love that He Himself sheds abroad in our hearts by the Holy Spirit who is given unto us (Romans 5:5).

Some of us who are possessed with the idea that our great business on earth is to carry out what has been called Pauline truth, need to remember that Pauline truth does not center in 1 Corinthians 5, but rises to its highest practical application in 1 Corinthians 13. We are not to neglect one passage in order to stress the other; both are right and proper in their own places.

We have been considering our attitudes toward our brothers in Christ and men of the world. Now in Colossians 3:15 we read of that which is distinctly personal: "Let the peace of God [some manuscripts read, the peace of Christ] rule in your hearts." It is the same peace that always filled His breast when He was here on earth, the same peace that is His as He sits on the throne of God in Heaven, far above all the storms of earth. We are to let that peace rule (or umpire) in our hearts.

We, as members of the body of Christ, are to seek things that make for peace in that body and things whereby we may edify one another. But in Colossians 3:15 Paul was clearly emphasizing that we should daily abide in the blessedness of communion with our risen Lord so that our hearts, like His own, may be kept in peace in spite of all we may be called on to pass through. Then we can fulfill the brief injunction, "Be ye thankful." Not the least of the sins of the unsaved is unthankfulness. Christians are called on to give thanks in every circumstance. Knowing that nothing except that which infinite Love allows can ever enter into the life of the believer, we give thanks "always for all things" (Ephesians 5:20).

In the King James version Colossians 3:16 is printed as follows: "Let the word of Christ dwell in you richly in all wisdom; teaching and admonishing one another in psalms and hymns and spiritual songs, singing with grace in your hearts to the Lord." Notice that the punctuation does not separate the three admonitions clearly and distinctly. The verse should be punctuated as follows: "Let the word of Christ dwell in you richly: in all wisdom teaching and admonishing one another: in psalms and hymns and spiritual songs singing with grace in your hearts to the Lord."

First we are told to let the word of Christ dwell in us richly. Colossians 3:16 is the only place in the New Testament where the expression "the word of Christ" is found. The expression suggests that the actual teaching of Christ—what was taught by Him personally when He was on earth or by the Spirit after He ascended to Heaven—is to dwell in full measure in all believers. Thus equipped and controlled by the truth, we will be able to bless and help others— "in all wisdom teaching and admonishing one another" (the second admonition). The truth we have been given is not to be kept to ourselves. We are to be ready to communicate.

Then in the third place, if we are controlled by the Word of God, our lives will be lyrical and our hearts will be filled with melody. "In psalms and hymns and spiritual songs" we will sing "with grace in our hearts to the Lord." Judah won a great victory when Jehoshaphat put the singers in the forefront of the army, and they returned to Jerusalem with joy. We read in Nehemiah 8:10, "The joy of the Lord is your strength." Depend on it, something is radically wrong with a Christian who can no longer praise and rejoice. Holiness and happiness go together.

The entire life of the believer is summed up as subjection to the Lord. Whatever he does, in action or speech, all is to be done "in the name of the Lord Jesus," through whom he gives thanks to God, even the Father (Colossians 3:17). There is no room for self-will or self-assertiveness in the life of the believer. Christ in His humiliation said, "I came down from heaven, not to do mine own will, but the will of him that sent me" (John 6:38), and the Christian, the new man, is left on earth to represent Christ and to do the will of the Lord, not to please himself.

Colossians 3:16-17 is intimately linked with Ephesians 5:18-20. The Ephesian passage speaks of being filled with the Spirit and the Colossian passage speaks of being filled with the Word, but the results are the same. A Word-filled Christian is a Spirit-filled Christian; that is, a Christian who is so controlled by the Word of God that it dominates his entire life, shows by his life that he is filled with the Holy Spirit. Careful comparison of these two passages might prevent a great deal of fanaticism and misunderstanding in regard to the fullness of blessing that every truly converted soul craves.

Human Ties (Colossians 3:18-25)

In these verses the Holy Spirit gives us instruction in regard to the sanctification of the natural, or earthly, relationships of the new man. It would be a great mistake to suppose, as some have done, that because we are members of the new creation we no longer need to consider ordinary human ties and responsibilities.

Galatians 3:28 tells us that in the new creation "there is neither Jew nor Greek, there is neither bond nor free, there is neither male nor female: for ye are all one in Christ Jesus." But while this is quite true, it is important to remember that our bodies still belong to the old creation and we will not be above natural relationships until the redemption of the body at the coming of our Lord Jesus Christ and our gathering together unto Him.

Even in the church, human distinctions between men and women are to be observed, as we are reminded in the Epistle to the Corinthians and the Epistles to Timothy and Titus. Some say that because there is neither male nor female in the new creation, we are to pay no attention to the divinely-given order pertaining to the respective places of man and woman in the church of God on earth. But to disregard the divine order is not only to go beyond Scripture; it is to disobey the Word of God. As long as we are subject to human limitations, we must recognize our human responsibilities and seek to carry them out in a Scriptural way in order to bring honor to the gospel of Christ. The new life is most blessedly displayed in circumstances that sometimes are hard for flesh and blood to endure, for where grace enables, it brings triumph.

The apostle Paul dealt very briefly in Colossians 3:18–4:1 with what he had devoted much more time to in the Epistle to the Ephesians. We should compare the instruction given in Colossians with the similar instruction given in Ephesians, and we should compare both of these Pauline passages to related teaching given in 1 Peter so that we may know all that God has revealed in regard to the principles that govern our behavior.

Note that in each of these Scripture passages the weaker is dealt with first, and then the stronger; the one subject to authority first, then the one in authority. So in Colossians, wives are addressed first and then husbands; children before fathers; and servants before masters. Let us carefully examine what the Holy Spirit says to each group.

In Colossians 3:18 we read, "Wives, submit yourselves unto your own husbands, as it is fit in the Lord." Where husband and wife are both Christians seeking to do the will of God and they have real mutual affection and esteem in their hearts, there will be no difficulty whatever in obeying an admonition such as this. If, however, the husband is a carnal, worldly, and unreasonable man, the wife will need true grace to yield loving obedience. Once the Christian woman has entered into a marriage, the only way she can conform to the will of God is to take the position of godly submission to the husband she has chosen.

We need to remember that the marriage relationship is divinely ordained and, as the old wedding ceremony puts it, "not to be lightly entered into." According to the Bible, marriage is not to be terminated easily either. The commitment is "for better, for worse, until death do us part," but these words are often flippantly uttered with no real conception of their seriousness. To seek to dissolve a marriage because of incompatibility of temperament is to fly in the face of the Word of the living God. Death, or what is equivalent to it (the infidelity of husband or wife), is the only Scriptural grounds for termination of a nuptial contract; in such a case the other party is free to remarry.

First Corinthians 7:11 implies that there may be circumstances in which no self-respecting woman could continue to live in her husband's home—if he is inflicting unspeakable cruelty, for example, or if there are abominable conditions that would be ruinous to soul and body alike—but if she departs, she is to remain unmarried, and if conditions change, she may be reconciled to her husband. As long as the woman remains with her husband, however, she is responsible to recognize his headship, for he is the one appointed by God to provide for the family. Even though conditions may sometimes be very distressing, she is to seek to win her wayward spouse by showing him the grace of Christ.

Today's loose ideas about easy divorce are bearing fearful fruit that will lead to more ungodliness as the end draws near. Eventually the corruption and vileness of the days before the flood and the unspeakable immoralities of the cities of the plain will be duplicated in Christendom. Of all this our blessed Lord warned us most solemnly.

Turning back to Colossians 3:18 we read again the words "as it is fit in the Lord." This part of the verse suggests that the submissive wife should display the gracious demeanor that always characterized our Lord while He was on the earth. Paul's words also suggest that the submission and obedience required is not the kind that would injure the wife's conscience or dishonor the Lord. She must always obey God first, for after all, hers is the submission of a wife, not a slave. It is loyalty to him who is her head that is enjoined.

In Colossians 3:19 we read, "Husbands, love your wives, and be not bitter against them." And how many husbands fail here! Imperiously demanding submission from their wives, they show little of the love of Christ in their dealings with those who are dependent on them. The Christian husband is to accept his place of headship as a sacred responsibility given to him by God Himself, and in the love of Christ he is to exercise his authority for the blessing of his home.

Just as some wives may be united to tyrannical and unreasonable men, so there are husbands who find that the one who seemed so docile and affectionate during their courtship is a veritable shrew and as unreasonable as it is possible to be. But still the husband is to love and care for her; he is to show all consideration, "giving honour unto the wife, as unto the weaker vessel" (1 Peter 3:7), without indulging in wrath or anger. God knew how petty and irritating some women's ways would be when He said to good men, "Be not bitter against them." In the power of the new life, one may display patience and grace under the most trying circumstances.

In Colossians 3:20 we read, "Children, obey your parents in all things: for this is well pleasing unto the Lord." In childhood days parents relate to their children the way God relates to the parents. Children who do not obey their parents, will not obey God when they reach adulthood. The natural heart is always rebellious against authority, and this rebellion has perhaps never been more strikingly demonstrated than in the democratic days in which we live. But Christian children should be examples of godly submission to father and mother or whoever may be in authority over them, and parents are responsible to instill the divine requirement of obedience in the hearts of their children. Young people who profess piety but ignore the principle of obedience are displaying utter insubordination to the One they own as Lord.

But notice in the next verse how carefully the Spirit of God guards the parent-child relationship; He says, "Fathers, provoke not your children to anger, lest they be discouraged" (Colossians 3:21). A parent may fill the growing boy or girl with indignation and contempt instead of drawing out the young heart in love and obedience. How easy it is for a man to forget the feelings of a child! But to instill resentment instead of tender affection in the heart of his little one is contrary to every instinct of the new man. The Christian father is to imitate Him who is our Father-God.

Paul went into the greatest detail when, beginning in Colossians 3:22, he addressed servants. When this Epistle was written, servants were slaves, not free men who served for wages. But if Paul's instructions were applicable to bondmen, how much more do they apply to those who have the privilege of selling their services and of terminating employment at will.

The apostle said there is no excuse whatever for surly, dishonest service because one's master or mistress is exasperating and unappreciative. But in the same exhortation Paul glorified the servant's lowly path, for his work for others can be done as unto the Lord Himself. Thus faithful service should be rendered not only when the master is watching, but also when no man is watching. The servant should perform his assigned tasks conscientiously "in singleness of heart, fearing God" (3:22).

If all his work is done as unto the Lord, the servant can be sure that He Himself will reward him accordingly. What an encouragement this was to the Roman or Greek slave whose faithful service was taken for granted.

If the Christian servant is treated cruelly or cheated out of the due reward of his labor, He can find comfort in remembering that God is taking note of it all and a day is coming when every wrong will be put right. Accounts that can never be settled fairly now will be settled fully then. Whether it is the servant who has been unfaithful or the master who has been unappreciative, the Lord will bring everything to light at His judgment seat—or in the case of the unsaved, at the great white throne—where every man will be judged according to his works.

We will see Paul's instructions to masters in Colossians 4:1.

CHAPTER FOUR
CHRIST, THE BELIEVER'S EXAMPLE

Marvelous Principles (Colossians 4:1)

It is unfortunate that the break between chapters 3 and 4 comes just where it does. It would seem far more suitable to include 4:1 in chapter 3 and let the next chapter begin with 4:2.

Colossians 4:1, which concludes the passage begun in 3:18, is a message to those in authority: "Masters, give unto your servants that which is just and equal; knowing that ye also have a Master in heaven." Paul was speaking to believers; ungodly masters could not have been expected to heed such an admonition. It was addressed to those who held the position of master in relation to their servants, but were themselves servants to their Master in Heaven. Such a master was urged to treat his servants as he would have the Lord treat him.

A Christian in a position of authority is to be characterized by fairness, giving to those beneath him that which is just. He should remember that his heavenly Master is observing him at all times and that when he is called to account for his actions, his relationship to his servants will be carefully reviewed and everything will be brought to light.

The rules that Paul stated so simply in Colossians 3:18–4:1 are marvelous principles. Only one who knows something of the conditions prevailing in the Roman empire at the time this Epistle was written can realize how revolutionary Paul's thoughts were. In those days wives, children, and slaves had practically no standing in the eyes of the law, unless their husbands, fathers, or masters desired to grant them recognition. But the glorious truth of the new man, the blessed unfolding of the revelation of the new creation, tinged with glory every earthly relationship in which the Christian was found. I am reminded of the blue border on the hem of the pious Israelite's garment. Even on the lower edge where his long flowing robe was most likely to touch the ground, this ribbon of blue could be seen; and blue, as we well know, is the heavenly color. The Israelite was to look at the ribbon and remember that he had confessed the Lord to be his God—the Lord who had said, "Ye shall be holy; for I am holy" (Leviticus 11:44). As he looked at the blue ribbon he was to remember his responsibility to honor and glorify the God of Heaven in his life on earth. Likewise we Christians are to reveal the heavenly character in every lawful relationship that God has established for the blessing of mankind during the present order of things.

A story is told about one of the dauphins of France who had an English tutor. This teacher found his royal pupil very difficult to handle. Proud, haughty, and impatient with restraint, the young man submitted unwillingly to schoolroom restrictions, and his foreign instructor was often at his wits' end about how to deal with him. One morning the tutor placed a purple rosette on the lapel of his pupil's jacket and said to him, "This is the royal color. As you wear it I want you to remember that you are the crown prince of France and that it is always incumbent on you to behave in a princely way. If you are willful or disobedient I will of course not attempt to punish you, as that is not in my province. I will simply point to the purple and you will understand what I mean: that I do not feel your behavior is worthy of a princely lad." The appeal to the purple!

May we not say that to us there is a similar appeal, but it is the appeal to the blue! Wives, husbands, children, fathers, servants, and masters—all alike are called on to reveal the holiness of Heaven, to display the heavenly character even in earthly relationships.

The power of the new life is wonderfully evident in these relationships. "Holding the Head" (Colossians 2:19) is not merely maintaining ecclesiastical truth. We are also "holding the Head" when we live holy, godly lives. The subjection of our hearts and minds to

Christ is nowhere more fully shown than in the way we live in our families and in the way we carry out our business and social responsibilities.

Concluding Exhortations (Colossians 4:2-6)

Paul exhorted the Colossians to "continue in prayer" (4:2). One of the most common sins among Christians today is prayerlessness. No doubt this statement could have been made throughout the centuries. And yet prayer is the life of the new man. We are again and again exhorted—and distinctly commanded—to pray.

- Men ought always to pray, and not to faint (Luke 18:1).
- Pray without ceasing (1 Thessalonians 5:17).
- Praying always with all prayer and supplication in the Spirit (Ephesians 6:18).
- Praying in the Holy Ghost (Jude 20).

To these examples could be added many similar expressions, each reminding us that "prayer is the Christian's vital breath" (James Montgomery). Just as one cannot be well and strong physically if he shuts himself up in a closed room where the sun never penetrates and pure air is unknown, one cannot have a happy, triumphant Christian experience if he neglects the spiritual exercise of prayer. The soul flourishes in an atmosphere of prayer.

People sometimes ask: "Why do we need to pray? If God is infinitely wise and infinitely good, as the Holy Scriptures declare Him to be, do any of His creatures need to petition Him for anything that is for their own good or the blessing of others? Is it not a higher and purer faith that leads one to ignore the exercise altogether and simply trust Him to do what is best?" Such reasoning shows how little the inquirers are acquainted with the Word of God and how little they understand the needs of the soul.

Prayer is, first of all, communion with God. Our blessed Lord Himself was seen again and again leaving the company of His disciples and going to a desert place on a mountainside, or to a garden, so that His spirit might be refreshed as He bowed in prayer alone with the Father. From such seasons of fellowship He returned to do His mightiest works and bear witness to the truth. And He is our great example. We too need to pray as much as we need to breathe. Our souls will languish without prayer, and our testimony will be utterly fruitless if we neglect our communion with God.

When the apostle told us to "continue in prayer," he did not mean that we are constantly to harass God in order to obtain what we think would be good for us or add to our happiness. Paul meant that we are to abide in a sense of His presence and in an awareness of our dependence on His bounty; we are to learn to talk to Him and wait quietly before Him so that we can hear His voice as He speaks to us.

We are assured that "if we ask any thing according to his will, he heareth us" (1 John 5:14). But because we are so ignorant and so shortsighted we need to remember that we are to leave the final decisions with Him who makes no mistakes. Without anxiety we may bring everything to God in "prayer and supplication with thanksgiving" (Philippians 4:6); we are bidden to make known our requests in childlike simplicity. Then, leaving the outcome in His hands, we can go forth in full confidence as our hearts say, "Thy will be done," since we know that He will "do exceeding abundantly above all that we ask or think" (Ephesians 3:20).

We need to be often reminded that we cannot pray as we should unless we are careful about our Christian walk, so Paul said not only to "continue in prayer," but also to "watch in the same." Matthew 26:41 says, "Watch and pray." Here are two commands that must never be separated. It is so easy to slip into carelessness, to become so entangled by worldly and unholy snares that we lose all spiritual discernment. When our souls are in such a condition, our prayers become selfish and then it is futile to think that we will obtain anything from the Lord. But when there is watchfulness and sobriety in our souls, when there is honest confession and self-judgment of failure, we can pray in full confidence, knowing that all hindrances have been removed.

In Colossians 4:2 as in Philippians 4:6, we are reminded that thanksgiving for past mercies should accompany prayer for present and future blessing. When we take God's good gifts for granted, our spiritual affection soon dries up. We become self-centered instead of Christ-centered and foolishly imagine that God is in some way bound to lavish His mercies on us whether we are grateful or not. In our dealings with one another we feel ingratitude keenly if kindness goes unacknowledged. Even when we give unselfishly we like appreciation, and a hearty thank-you makes us all the more ready to minister again when there is a need. Likewise our God finds joy in His people's praises. He loves to give and He delights in our appreciation of His benefits.

Colossians 4:3 turns our attention from thanksgiving to intercession. Paul, unquestionably the greatest preacher and teacher that the Christian dispensation has known, was not above requesting the prayers of the people of God. He felt his need of their prayer-help, for he did not think that because he was in jail his work was over. Although he was unable to face multitudes in public places as in past years, he was always on the lookout for chances to serve, and he wanted the saints to join with him in prayer that even in his prison cell "a door of utterance" would open (Colossians 4:3).

How natural it would have been for him to give up in despair and settle down in utter discouragement or to endure the long, weary months of imprisonment passively, simply taking it for granted that he would not be able to spread the gospel again until he was freed. But Paul was of another mind entirely. His circumstances did not indicate that God had forsaken him or set him to one side. He was eagerly looking for fresh opportunities to advance on the enemy.

Just before the first battle of the Marne in World War I, Marshal Ferdinand Foch, the great French general, reported: "My center is giving; my left wing is retreating; the situation is excellent; I am attacking." This was not mere military bombast, for the marshal realized that apparent defeat could be turned into victory by acting with resolution and alacrity at the very moment when the enemy seemed to be triumphant.

Doubtless the devil thought he had gained a great advantage when he shut Paul up in prison, but from that prison cell came at least four of the church epistles and some of the pastoral letters, which have been the means of untold blessing to millions throughout the centuries. And the gospel went out from that cell too: first to the prison guards, and through them to many more in caesar's palace who might not otherwise have been reached. How important it is not to give ground to Satan, but in prayer and faith to turn every defeat into a victory; assured that our great Captain knows no retreat, we can seize the opportunity and advance against the foe. We spend so much time halting between two opinions (1 Kings 18:21), debating what we should do, and doing nothing. We need the grace of decision that will enable us to seize the opportune moment and take immediate action in the fear of God. And so Paul told us to "walk in wisdom toward them that are without, redeeming the time" (Colossians 4:5). As we interact with men of the world, we need to remember that we may have chances to share the gospel with them, and that opportunities once given may never come again. It is tremendously important to buy up such privileges of service, for the believer's works will be reviewed at the judgment seat of Christ.

We meet men once, perhaps never to see them again, and while it is perfectly true that we cannot be forever pestering people about what they would call our religious notions, it is wise to be on the lookout for openings to minister Christ to their souls. The day of grace is fast passing away.

> To each man's life there comes a time supreme,
>   One day, one night, one morning, or one noon,
>   One freighted hour, one moment opportune,
> One rift through which sublime fulfillments gleam,
> One space when faith goes tiding with the stream,
>   One *Once* in balance 'twixt Too Late, Too Soon,
>   And ready for the passing instant's boon
> To tip in favor of uncertain beam.

> Ah, happy he who, knowing how to wait,
>   Knows also how to watch, and work, and stand,
> On Life's broad deck alert, and at the prow
> To seize the passing moment, big with fate,
>   From Opportunity's extended hand,
> When the great clock of Destiny strikes *now!*

But if we want our testimony really to count, we must be careful that our walk agrees with our speech. Careless behavior in the company of worldlings will leave the impression that we do not believe the tremendous truths that we are urging them to accept. How circumspect preachers need to be! The world, so quick to judge, will only turn away with disgust from a man who is serious on the platform but frivolous among men. He who is solemn as he preaches of divine realities, but a buffoon when socializing, need not think that he will make any permanent impression for good on the hearts and consciences of those among whom he mingles. Many a servant of Christ has cheapened himself and his ministry by coming down to the level of natural men who do not know the power of the new life; in his anxiety to be a good mixer—sincerely hoping thereby to gain acceptance of his message—he has found to his sorrow that he has paid too high a price for his popularity.

A friend once told me about two preachers. One was perhaps a bit unduly serious. No one can be too sober as he faces the realities of eternity, but the man in question was too stern to make friends readily among those whom he wished to help. The other preacher was the very soul of cordiality. He would tell a good story, smoke a good cigar, and make himself hail-fellow-well-met with everyone he contacted. Speaking of him, my friend said, "Dr. — is a fine fellow. I do enjoy an hour in his company; he makes me forget all my troubles, but," he added thoughtfully, "if I were dying, I'd rather have Mr. — come and pray with me."

Let us not forfeit our high and holy calling as Christ's representatives in order to obtain popularity among men who have little relish for divine things. I do not mean that we should be disagreeable in our behavior or conversation, for we are told, "Let your speech be alway with grace, seasoned with salt, that ye may know how ye ought to answer every man" (Colossians 4:6).

Gracious speech flows from a heart established in the grace of God. The psalmist wrote of Jesus, "Grace is poured into thy lips" (Psalm 45:2). And Psalm 18:35 says, "Thy gentleness hath made me great." But this gentleness did not make Jesus indifferent to evil or unfaithful in dealing with those who needed rebuke.

There is always the danger that a gracious man will become a weak man, lacking the courage to speak out faithfully when the occasion demands it. When Christ's honor is at stake or when we realize a brother is standing in a dangerous place, we need to season our gracious speech with salt. Salt suggests the preservative power of faithfulness and we are all our brothers' keepers to a certain extent. While nothing is more contrary to the spirit of Christ than an arrogant, fault-finding spirit, there are times when Leviticus 19:17 applies: "Thou shalt in any wise rebuke thy neighbor, and not suffer sin upon him."

We need the salt of righteousness so that we will know how to speak to every man. To perfect ourselves in this grace, we need to live more in company with the Lord Jesus Christ. If we follow Him through the Gospels in His wondrous ministry here on earth, we will see how marvelously He met each individual case. As F. W. Grant said, "Our Lord had no stereotyped method of dealing with souls." He did not talk to the woman at the well the same way He addressed Nicodemus, a ruler of the Jews. Christ probed the depths of each heart and ministered according to its need.

His devoted follower, the apostle Paul, the author of this divinely inspired letter to the Colossians, tried to do the same. He said, "I am made all things to all men, that I might by all means save some" (1 Corinthians 9:22). In Jewish synagogues he reasoned on the basis of Scripture—like the most able rabbi or doctor of the law. When Paul stood on Mars Hill among the Athenian philosophers, he spoke like a master of rhetoric and showed full acquaintance with Greek thought and literature; but he spoke "not as pleasing men, but God, which trieth our hearts" (1 Thessalonians 2:4) until his great oration was interrupted by the excited throng who spurned the idea of the resurrection of the body. Addressing the idolaters of Lycaonia, the apostle met them on their own ground and appealed to nature as evidence of a Creator as he sought to turn them away from their vanities and draw their hearts to nature's God.

How different were both the Master and His servant Paul from many who today seem to pride themselves on their outspokenness and indifference to the views and opinions of others. Is it any wonder that men turn from them in disgust and refuse to listen to what seems to be the dogmatic utterances of self-centered egotists? On the other hand, there are those who seek to be gracious, but lack faithfulness; they gloss over wrong doctrine and evil in the lives of their hearers rather than run the risk of giving offense. How much divine wisdom is needed and how close must the servant keep to the Master if he would know how "to answer every man"!

Closing Remarks (Colossians 4:7-18)

This last passage, though somewhat lengthy, does not require very much in the way of either exposition or explanation. It is interesting, however, to compare references to people mentioned here with references to the same people in other Epistles.

We do not know much about Tychicus, who is mentioned in Colossians 4:7, except that in Ephesians 6:21-22 he is spoken of in almost the same terms. It is evident that the apostle had implicit confidence in him. Paul spoke of him in both Epistles as a beloved brother and faithful minister, and in Colossians added a third expression, "fellowservant in the Lord."

Beloved and yet faithful—what a rare but blessed combination! So often men who seek to be faithful become almost unconsciously stern and ungracious, thereby forfeiting the tender affection of the people of God. These stern individuals may be respected as men of principle who can be depended on to do and say the righteous thing at any cost, but they may show very little real concern for the peace of mind or comfort of heart of those who disagree with them. On the other hand, many a beloved brother purchases the affectionate regard of the saints at the cost of faithfulness to truth. It is far better to be true to Christ and His Word, and thus have His approval, than to be approved of men and loved because of weakness in enforcing what is in accordance with truth.

Tychicus evidently went to neither extreme. He was undoubtedly a lovable man because of his gracious demeanor and his tender solicitude for the welfare of the saints, but at the same time he was faithful in ministering the Word of God, rebuking iniquity and also comforting the penitent. Such men are rarer than we realize. In them we see the delightful combination of the shepherd's heart and the prophet's spirit. Timothy and Tychicus were very much alike in character. Both were loyal to the Word of God and both sought the comfort and blessing of the people of God.

In Colossians 4:9 Onesimus is spoken of in similar terms. Although he did not have the same gifts as Tychicus, Onesimus was a "faithful and beloved brother." We know much more about him than we know about some of the others mentioned in Colossians 4. The brief letter to Philemon tells us a great deal about the history of Onesimus. He had been a dishonest runaway slave. He had robbed his master (Philemon) and apparently had wasted his ill-gotten gains before he was brought to Christ through Paul's ministry in Rome. It was also through Paul that Philemon had been converted, so his extension of mercy to the thieving slave is a wondrous picture of sovereign grace.

> Sov'reign grace o'er sin abounding;
> Ransomed souls the tidings swell!
> 'Tis a deep that knows no sounding;
> Who its length and breadth can tell?
> On its glories
> Let my soul forever dwell.

After Onesimus was brought to Christ, Paul sent him back to his master and offered to become the slave's surety. The apostle wrote to Philemon: "If thou count me therefore a partner, receive him as myself. If he hath wronged thee, or oweth thee ought, put that on mine account; I Paul have written it with mine own hand, I will repay it" (17-19). What a gospel picture this is, for Christ assumed the responsibilities of the penitent sinner. "We are all God's Onesimuses," said Luther. Christ paid our debt that we might be accepted in Him by God. "He bore on the tree, the sentence for me, / And now both the Surety and sinner are free." Thus redeemed, we have the happy privilege of serving Him in glorious liberty and saying with the psalmist, "Truly I am thy servant....Thou hast loosed my bonds" (Psalm 116:16).

Aristarchus is mentioned in Colossians 4:10 as Paul's "fellow-prisoner." We read in Acts 19:29 that he was a Macedonian traveling with Paul and that he endangered his very life on behalf of the gospel at the time of the uproar in Ephesus. Aristarchus is also mentioned in Philemon 24 as one of the apostle's "fellowlabourers." His name implies that he was a member of the upper class, an aristocrat who for the sake of the kingdom of God renounced his place of prominence in the world to become a bondsman of Jesus Christ.

We can be glad to see the affectionate way in which Paul wrote of Marcus, the nephew of Barnabas (Colossians 4:10). Years before, this young man had been the cause of serious contention between Paul and Barnabas: Paul lost confidence in John Mark because, upon completion of the evangelistic tour in Cyprus, he left the work and returned to his mother in Jerusalem. Barnabas, kindly in spirit and evidently moved by natural affection, wanted to give the unfaithful helper a second chance, but Paul was obdurate. He felt he could not afford to jeopardize the success of their work by again taking a weakling with them. Which one—Paul or Barnabas—really had the mind of God, we are not told; but we are thankful indeed to find that Mark became a trusted and honored man of God.

First Peter 5:13 indicates that Mark was a companion to Peter. We know that Mark became dear to Paul, as well as to his uncle Barnabas, for the apostle referred to the young man as a fellow laborer in Philemon 24 and asked Timothy to bring Mark to him in 2 Timothy 4:11. The fact that Mark needed the recommendation given parenthetically in Colossians 4:10 seems to imply that at the time the Epistle was written there were still some who had reservations about him, but the apostle's comment would remove all doubts.

Colossians 4:11 refers to "Jesus, which is called Justus." His name might well remind us of the humiliation that our blessed Lord experienced when in grace He stooped to become a man in order to give His life for sinners. To us there is only one Jesus. That name is now "above every name" (Philippians 2:9) and it shines resplendent in highest glory; unique and precious, it is a name with which no other can ever be compared. But we need to remember that *Jesus* is the equivalent of the Hebrew *Joshua,* a name in common use when our Lord was here on earth. And so a brother otherwise unknown bore the same name as his Savior. Moreover he was surnamed "the

Just." This title was given to men because of their recognized integrity, as in the case of Joseph Barsabas of Acts 1:23 and the otherwise unknown Justus of Acts 18:7.

There is something peculiarly significant in the way the apostle eulogized the brothers whose greetings he conveyed to the Colossians. "These only," he said, "are my fellow workers unto the kingdom of God, which have been a comfort unto me" (4:11). It is evident that then as now, gift and grace did not necessarily go together. There were other believers who were perhaps energetic enough in service, but who were anything but brotherly in their attitude toward Paul.

We have already read the apostle's praise of Epaphras in Colossians 1:7. It was he who had come from Colossae to acquaint Paul with conditions in the church there. In 4:12 the apostle drew special attention to the man's fervency in prayer. Epaphras must also have had some ability as a preacher and teacher, for it was through his ministry that the Colossians had been won to Christ and the local church had been established; but his greatest ministry was evidently one of laboring in prayer. His earnest supplication was that the saints might know the truth in all its fullness and that in practical experience they might "stand perfect [full-grown] and complete [filled full] in all the will of God." Paul joined in this prayer, as we have seen in Colossians 1:9. Epaphras had not confined his ministry or interest to Colossae; he bore in his heart, with the same intense zeal, the neighboring assemblies of believers in Laodicea and Hierapolis.

In Colossians 4:14 we read, "Luke, the beloved physician, and Demas, greet you." But in 2 Timothy 4:10-11 the apostle said, "Demas hath forsaken me, having loved this present world, and is departed unto Thessalonica....Only Luke is with me." It is most pathetic to compare the two references to Demas.

On the occasion of Paul's second imprisonment, Demas left the apostle in his hour of need and went off to Thessalonica. Evidently he found the itinerant preacher's lot too hard. There is no hint that Demas plunged into a life of sin and he may have gone into some respectable business, but the Holy Ghost relentlessly exposed the hidden springs of his changed behavior: he "loved this present world." Once Demas and Luke were, so it seems, intimately associated, for the two names are found together in both Colossians 4:14 and Philemon 24, but at the time 2 Timothy was written, they were no longer joined in devoted service. Demas had chosen an easier path.

As intimated in Acts 16, where the pronoun changes from "they" in verse 8 to "we" in verse 10, Luke joined the missionary party at Troas. From the day he became a member of Paul's company, "the beloved physician" was one of the apostle's most devoted helpers. Luke remained with Paul to the end and possibly saw him martyred.

In Colossians 4:15 salutations were sent to the Laodicean brethren, especially Nymphas, who was evidently prominent among them. It seems that the Christians of Laodicea met in his house for worship.

We gather from Colossians 4:16 that the apostolic letters were circulated among the early churches. The Colossian Epistle was to be read locally and in the assembly of the Laodicean believers. The Laodiceans were to forward another letter to Colossae. This Epistle "from" Laodicea (observe that the preposition is *from,* not *to*) is probably our Epistle to the Ephesians, which is generally regarded as a circular letter that went first to Ephesus and then to other churches in the Roman proconsular province of Asia. Thus the Ephesian letter came to Colossae from Laodicea.

Colossians 4:17 has a special admonition for Archippus, who is also mentioned in Philemon 2. Apparently Archippus was ministering at Colossae, but he had a tendency not uncommon in some young preachers to settle down comfortably and take things easily. Promptness and energy are as important in spiritual service as in anything else.

An incident involving two leading generals of the southern confederacy might speak well to every servant of Christ. General Robert E. Lee once sent word to General Stonewall Jackson that he would be glad to talk with him at his convenience on some matter of no great urgency. Even though the weather was most inclement, General Jackson instantly rode to headquarters. When General Lee expressed surprise at seeing him, Jackson exclaimed, "General Lee's slightest wish is a supreme command to me, and I always take pleasure in prompt obedience." It is to be hoped that this same spirit took hold of Archippus and that he profited from the prodding of the aged apostle.

Colossians 4:18 indicates that in accordance with his usual custom, Paul signed the Epistle with his own hand. Tychicus and Onesimus may have transcribed the letter, but the apostle appended his signature. How much would one give to have an autographed copy of this or any of his other letters!

Paul's final command was, "Remember my bonds." He wanted his readers to remember his chains so that they would be stirred to pray and so that they would keep in mind that the servant's path is one of suffering and rejection.

The apostle closed his Colossian letter with the customary benediction, "Grace be with you. Amen." Second Thessalonians 3:17-18 tells us that this benediction is the token that an Epistle is genuinely Paul's, and in every one of the thirteen letters that bear his name and in the anonymous letter to the Hebrews we see some message about grace at the end. Paul was pre-eminently the apostle of *grace,* and it is not surprising that this precious word is the secret mark authenticating every letter. May that grace abound in us as it already has abounded toward us through the abundant mercy of our God.

> Grace is the sweetest sound
>> That ever reached our ears,
> When conscience charged and Justice frowned,
>> 'Twas grace removed our fears!

We began with grace, we are kept by grace, and it is grace that will bring us home at last.

AUTHOR BIOGRAPHY

HENRY ALLAN IRONSIDE, one of this century's greatest preachers, was born in Toronto, Canada, on October 14, 1876. He lived his life by faith; his needs at crucial moments were met in the most remarkable ways.

Though his classes stopped with grammar school, his fondness for reading and an incredibly retentive memory put learning to use. His scholarship was well recognized in academic circles with Wheaton College awarding an honorary Litt.D. in 1930 and Bob Jones University an honorary D.D. in 1942. Dr. Ironside was also appointed to the boards of numerous Bible institutes, seminaries, and Christian organizations.

"HAI" lived to preach and he did so widely throughout the United States and abroad. E. Schuyler English, in his biography of Ironside, revealed that during 1948, the year HAI was 72, and in spite of failing eyesight, he "gave 569 addresses, besides participating in many other ways." In his eighteen years at Chicago's Moody Memorial Church, his only pastorate, every Sunday but two had at least one profession of faith in Christ.

H. A. Ironside went to be with the Lord on January 15, 1951. Throughout his ministry, he authored expositions on 51 books of the Bible and through the great clarity of his messages led hundreds of thousands, worldwide, to a knowledge of God's Word. His words are as fresh and meaningful today as when first preached.

The official biography of Dr. Ironside, *H. A. Ironside: Ordained of the Lord*, is available from the publisher.

THE WRITTEN MINISTRY OF
H. A. IRONSIDE

Expositions

Joshua
Ezra
Nehemiah
Esther
Psalms (1-41 only)
Proverbs
Song of Solomon
Isaiah
Jeremiah
Lamentations
Ezekiel
Daniel
The Minor Prophets
Matthew
Mark
Luke
John

Acts
Romans
1 & 2 Corinthians
Galatians
Ephesians
Philippians
Colossians
1 & 2 Thessalonians
1 & 2 Timothy
Titus
Philemon
Hebrews
James
1 & 2 Peter
1,2, & 3 John
Jude
Revelation

Doctrinal Works

Baptism
Death and Afterward
Eternal Security of the Believer
Holiness: The False and
the True
The Holy Trinity

Letters to a Roman Catholic
Priest
The Levitical Offerings
Not Wrath But Rapture
Wrongly Dividing the Word
of Truth

Historical Works

The Four Hundred Silent Years
A Historical Sketch of the Brethren Movement

Other works by the author are brought back into print from time to time. All of this material is available from your local Christian bookstore or from the publisher.